How to Become a Profitable Trader

Trading Secrets, Tools, Strategies, and Price Action Techniques for Beginners

Peter E. James

Disclaimer:

The information in this book is provided for educational and entertainment purposes only. While every effort has been made to ensure accuracy, no warranties are declared or implied. The author is not liable for any damages or losses resulting from the use of this information. Please consult a licensed professional before applying any techniques discussed in this book.

Trading involves risk. This information is for educational purposes only and should not be considered financial advice

Table of Contents

Stock Trading with Price Action
Cryptocurrency Trading with Price Action

Introduction to Price Action Trading

My Journey from Market Mishaps to Price Action Profits

I'll never forget the sinking feeling in my stomach as I watched my trading account dwindle, trade after trade. It was 2018, and I was fresh out of university, brimming with ambition and a naive confidence that I could conquer the financial markets. Armed with a few online tutorials and a demo account that had shown some promise, I dove headfirst into the world of forex trading.

At first, the thrill of the market was intoxicating. The charts danced before my eyes, each flicker of price a potential opportunity. I followed every tip I could find, chased every hot stock, and jumped on every trend. I felt like I was on the cusp of something big.

But reality soon set in. My early wins turned into a string of losses. I'd enter trades based on gut feelings or news headlines, only to watch the market turn against me. I'd hold onto losing positions, hoping for a reversal that never came. I'd double down on bad trades, trying to recoup my losses, only to dig myself deeper into a hole.

The emotional toll was immense. Each loss chipped away at my confidence, replacing it with doubt and anxiety. I'd spend sleepless nights staring at charts, replaying my mistakes, and wondering where I'd gone wrong. My once-promising trading account was now a shadow of its former self.

One day, after a particularly devastating loss, I realized I needed a change. I couldn't keep trading this way; it was unsustainable, both financially and emotionally. I began scouring the internet for a better approach, something that would give me a real edge in the markets.

That's when I stumbled upon price action trading. At first, it seemed too simple. No fancy indicators, no complex algorithms, just the raw price data on the chart. But as I delved deeper, I realized the elegance and power of this approach.

Price action trading taught me to read the market's language, to understand the psychology behind the price movements. I learned to identify key support and resistance levels, to spot trend reversals, and to time my entries and exits with precision. It was like learning a new language, and with each new concept I grasped, my confidence grew.

I started small, testing my newfound knowledge on a demo account. Slowly but surely, I began to see results. My trades were more consistent, my losses were smaller, and my wins were more frequent. The emotional rollercoaster I'd been on for so long finally started to level out.

It wasn't an overnight transformation. There were still setbacks and learning curves, but I was now equipped with a solid foundation and a clear methodology. I was no longer trading blindly; I was making informed decisions based on a deep understanding of the market.

Today, I'm a profitable trader. I'm not a millionaire, but I consistently make money in the markets. More importantly, I've regained my confidence and my passion for trading. I no longer fear the markets; I embrace them.

Price action trading has been my salvation. It's given me the tools and the mindset to succeed in a field where so many fail. If you're struggling in the markets, I urge you to give price action a try. It might just change your trading life, as it did mine.

The Essence of Price Action: The Market Speaks

Imagine the financial market as a grand theater, where a complex drama unfolds every second. Stocks, currencies, commodities – each a character in this play, their movements choreographed by an intricate web of supply and demand, fear and greed, and countless other forces. Technical indicators, fundamental analysis, and news headlines often try to interpret this drama, but they can be akin to noisy audience members, each offering their own biased commentary.

Price action trading, however, takes a different approach. It cuts through the noise and focuses on the most fundamental element: the price itself. Just like a skilled detective who observes footprints and fingerprints at a crime scene, a price action trader scrutinizes the charts, looking for clues left behind by the market's participants. These clues are manifested in the patterns formed by price bars or candlesticks, revealing the underlying dynamics of the market.

Price action, therefore, is the "language" of the market, a raw and unfiltered record of its every move. By mastering this language, traders can gain a profound understanding of market sentiment, anticipate potential turning points, and make informed trading decisions.

The Allure of Price Action Trading: Simplicity and Universality

Price action trading is appealing for several reasons:

Simplicity: Unlike complex technical indicators that often require extensive calculations and interpretations, price action trading relies on the naked chart. This simplicity makes it accessible to traders of all levels, from beginners to seasoned professionals.

Universality: Price action principles can be applied across all markets, including stocks, forex, commodities, and cryptocurrencies. This versatility allows traders to adapt their strategies to different asset classes and market conditions.

Self-Reliance: By focusing on price action, traders become less dependent on external sources of information, such as news or expert opinions. This self-reliance fosters independent thinking and empowers traders to make their own judgments.

Timelessness: The principles of price action have remained largely unchanged for centuries. While markets may evolve, human psychology and the underlying forces of supply and demand remain constant. This timelessness makes price action trading a reliable approach even in the face of ever-changing market dynamics.

Key Concepts in Price Action Trading

To navigate the world of price action, traders must familiarize themselves with a few key concepts:

- Support and Resistance: These are price levels where buying or selling pressure is expected to be strong enough to halt or reverse a price trend. Support acts as a floor, preventing prices from falling further, while resistance acts as a ceiling, preventing prices from rising further.
- Trend: A trend represents the overall direction of the market, whether it is moving upwards (uptrend), downwards (downtrend), or sideways (sideways trend). Identifying the trend is crucial for determining the appropriate trading strategy.
- Candlestick Patterns: Candlestick charts offer a visual representation of price action, with each candlestick depicting the opening, closing, high, and low prices for a given period. Certain candlestick patterns, such as doji or engulfing patterns, can provide valuable insights into potential market reversals or continuations.
- Chart Patterns: Chart patterns, such as head and shoulders or triangles, are formed by the collective movement of price bars or candlesticks over time. These patterns can signal potential

trend reversals or continuations, offering traders opportunities to enter or exit trades.

- Price Action Trading Strategies: A wide array of trading strategies can be built upon the foundation of price action. Some popular examples include:

Trend following: This strategy aims to capture profits by riding the prevailing trend. Traders enter long positions in an uptrend and short positions in a downtrend.

Breakout trading: This strategy seeks to capitalize on price breakouts from established support or resistance levels. Traders enter trades in the direction of the breakout, anticipating a strong price move.

Reversal trading: This strategy aims to identify potential trend reversals and enter trades at the early stages of a new trend. Traders look for candlestick patterns, chart patterns, or other price action signals that suggest a change in market direction.

The Importance of Risk Management

While price action trading offers a powerful approach to understanding and profiting from the markets, it is crucial to remember that trading always involves risk. No trading strategy, no matter how well-designed, can guarantee profits. Therefore, effective risk management is essential for any trader, regardless of their experience level.

Risk management involves carefully planning and executing trades to limit potential losses. This can include setting stop-loss orders to automatically exit trades if they move against you, diversifying your portfolio to spread risk across different asset classes, and never risking more than you can afford to lose.

By combining a solid understanding of price action with sound risk management principles, traders can increase their chances of success in the markets. Remember, trading is a journey, not a destination. It requires continuous learning, adaptation, and discipline. But with dedication and perseverance, you can unlock the secrets of price action and embark on a rewarding path towards profitable trading.

The Mindset of a Successful Price Action Trader

In addition to technical skills and risk management, successful price action traders possess a certain mindset that sets them apart. This mindset includes:

Patience: The markets rarely move in a straight line. Price action traders understand the importance of waiting for the right opportunities to present themselves, rather than chasing every potential trade.

Discipline: Sticking to a well-defined trading plan and avoiding impulsive decisions is crucial for long-term success. Price action traders develop the discipline to execute their strategies consistently, even in the face of market volatility.

Adaptability: Markets are constantly evolving, and successful traders must be willing to adapt their strategies accordingly. Price action traders stay abreast of market developments and adjust their approach as needed.

Emotional Control: Fear and greed are powerful emotions that can cloud judgment and lead to poor trading decisions. Price action traders learn to manage their emotions and maintain a rational approach, even in stressful situations.

Continuous Learning: The markets are a vast and complex ecosystem, and there is always more to learn. Successful price action traders embrace a lifelong learning mindset, constantly seeking to improve their skills and knowledge.

What is Price Action Trading?

Price action trading, at its core, is the art of interpreting the raw price movements of a financial instrument. It's about observing the footprints left by buyers and sellers in the market, deciphering their intentions, and using that knowledge to anticipate future price movements. In essence, it's about reading the market's language, without the need for translation through indicators or news.

The Essence of Price Action

Imagine the market as a bustling auction house. Buyers and sellers are constantly vying for control, pushing prices up or down depending on their collective strength. Price action trading focuses solely on these price movements, represented graphically on a chart as bars or candlesticks. Each bar or candlestick tells a story – the opening price, the closing price, the high and the low of a specific time period. By studying these formations, traders can gauge the balance of power between buyers and sellers and make informed decisions.

Why Price Action?

Purity of Information: Price action is the most direct reflection of market sentiment. It's unfiltered, unbiased, and free from the lag or potential inaccuracies of indicators derived from price.

Universality: The principles of price action apply across all markets – stocks, forex, commodities, cryptocurrencies. The patterns and formations you learn in one market can be applied to others.

Self-Reliance: Price action empowers traders to make independent decisions. You're not reliant on external signals or the opinions of others. You become your own analyst.

Adaptability: Markets are dynamic, constantly evolving. Price action trading equips you with the tools to adapt to any market condition. You learn to read the market as it is, not as you wish it to be.

The Building Blocks of Price Action

Support and Resistance: These are price levels where buying or selling pressure is expected to be strong enough to halt or reverse a trend. They act as floors and ceilings in the market.

Trendlines: These are lines drawn connecting a series of highs or lows, revealing the direction and strength of a trend.

Candlestick Patterns: These are specific formations of candlesticks that provide clues about potential reversals or continuations of trends.

Chart Patterns: These are larger formations on a chart, such as triangles or head and shoulders patterns, that suggest potential breakouts or reversals.

The Mindset of a Price Action Trader

Patience: Price action trading is not about chasing every move. It's about waiting for the right setup, the high-probability trade.

Discipline: Sticking to your trading plan, even when emotions run high, is crucial. Price action provides the clarity, but discipline ensures its execution.

Objectivity: The market doesn't care about your opinions or biases. A price action trader learns to observe the market objectively, without letting emotions cloud their judgment.

Continuous Learning: The market is a lifelong teacher. A price action trader is always seeking to improve their understanding, refine their strategies, and adapt to new market conditions.

Getting Started with Price Action Trading

1. Learn the Basics: Familiarize yourself with the key concepts – support and resistance, trendlines, candlestick patterns, and chart patterns.

2. Practice on a Demo Account: Apply your knowledge in a risk-free environment. Experiment with different strategies and see what works for you.

3. Develop a Trading Plan: Define your entry and exit criteria, risk management rules, and overall trading strategy.

4. Start Small: When you transition to live trading, start with small positions and gradually increase your size as you gain confidence and experience.

5. Review and Refine: Analyze your trades, identify your strengths and weaknesses, and continuously refine your approach.

The Power of Price Action

Price action trading is not a get-rich-quick scheme. It requires dedication, discipline, and a willingness to learn from both successes and failures. But for those who master its principles, it offers a path to consistent profitability and a deep understanding of the market's inner workings. It's about seeing beyond the noise, recognizing the underlying patterns, and making informed decisions based on the purest form of market data – price action.

Remember: The market is a complex and ever-changing entity. There's no single "right" way to trade. Price action provides a powerful framework, but it's up to you to develop your own style, adapt to market conditions, and continuously refine your approach. The journey may be challenging, but the rewards – financial independence, self-reliance, and a deep connection to the market – are well worth the effort.

Benefits of Price Action Trading

In the dynamic world of trading, where countless strategies and indicators vie for attention, price action trading stands as a beacon of simplicity and effectiveness. At its core, price action trading involves analyzing the raw price movements of a financial instrument, deciphering the market's story as it unfolds on the chart. For beginners especially, the benefits of embracing this approach are manifold, providing a solid foundation for navigating the complexities of the markets and potentially achieving consistent profitability.

1. Unfiltered Market Insights

One of the most compelling benefits of price action trading is its reliance on raw, unfiltered market data. Unlike strategies that depend on lagging indicators or external news sources, price action traders focus solely on the price itself - the purest reflection of supply and demand in the market. By studying price charts, traders gain direct insights into the ongoing battle between buyers and sellers, allowing them to make informed decisions based on real-time market dynamics.

2. Versatility Across Markets and Timeframes

Price action trading is inherently versatile, applicable across a wide range of financial markets and timeframes. Whether you're interested in stocks, forex, commodities, or cryptocurrencies, the principles of price action remain consistent. Additionally, price action patterns and strategies can be adapted to suit various trading styles, from short-term scalping to long-term investing. This adaptability empowers traders to find a niche that aligns with their risk tolerance and investment goals.

3. A Focus on Simplicity

In a world of complex algorithms and sophisticated trading systems, price action trading offers a refreshing sense of simplicity. By stripping away extraneous indicators and relying on the naked price chart, traders can develop a clear and concise understanding of market behavior. This focus on simplicity reduces cognitive overload and allows traders to make decisions with clarity and confidence.

4. Self-Reliance and Independence

Price action trading fosters a sense of self-reliance and independence. Unlike traders who rely on external signals or the opinions of others, price action traders develop their own analytical skills and decision-making frameworks. This autonomy empowers traders to take ownership of their trades and avoid the pitfalls of blindly following the crowd.

5. Enhanced Risk Management

Effective risk management is crucial for long-term trading success, and price action trading offers unique advantages in this area. By identifying key support and resistance levels, traders can strategically place stop-loss orders to limit potential losses. Moreover, price action signals can provide valuable insights into potential trend reversals or breakouts, allowing traders to manage their positions proactively and protect their capital.

6. Adaptability to Changing Market Conditions

Financial markets are constantly evolving, and successful traders must be able to adapt to changing conditions. Price action trading excels in this regard, as it provides a real-time view of market sentiment and trend dynamics. By focusing on the current price action, traders can quickly identify shifts in market behavior and adjust their strategies accordingly.

7. A Foundation for Lifelong Learning

Price action trading is not simply a collection of techniques but a holistic approach to understanding the markets. As traders delve deeper into the study of price action, they embark on a journey of continuous learning and self-improvement. This ongoing education process can lead to greater market awareness, refined analytical skills, and ultimately, increased profitability.

8. Accessibility for Beginners

While price action trading can be complex at advanced levels, its core principles are accessible to beginners. With a basic understanding of chart patterns, support and resistance, and trend analysis, novice traders can start applying price action concepts to their trading strategies. This low barrier to entry makes price action trading an attractive option for those new to the markets.

9. Cost-Effectiveness

Compared to other trading strategies that may require expensive software or subscriptions to data feeds, price action trading is relatively cost-effective. All you need is a basic charting platform and a willingness to learn. This affordability makes price action trading a viable option for traders with limited capital.

10. A Path to Consistent Profitability

Ultimately, the most significant benefit of price action trading is its potential to lead to consistent profitability. By mastering the art of reading the market's language through price action, traders can develop a trading edge that sets them apart from the majority. While success in trading requires discipline, patience, and continuous learning, price action trading provides a solid foundation for achieving long-term financial goals.

Additional Tips for Beginners:

Start with the Basics: Focus on mastering basic price action concepts like support and resistance, trend lines, and candlestick patterns before moving on to more advanced techniques.

Practice on a Demo Account: Use a demo account to practice your price action skills without risking real money. This will allow you to experiment and refine your strategies in a risk-free environment.

Keep a Trading Journal: Document your trades, including your analysis, entry and exit points, and the outcome. This will help you track your progress and identify areas for improvement.

Be Patient and Disciplined: Successful trading takes time and dedication. Don't expect to become an overnight expert. Stick to your plan, manage your risk, and be patient with the process.

Never Stop Learning: The markets are constantly evolving, so it's important to continue learning and adapting. Read books, attend webinars, and connect with other traders to stay ahead of the curve.

Remember, price action trading is a journey, not a destination. By embracing the benefits outlined in this chapter and committing to continuous learning, you can develop the skills and confidence needed to navigate the markets and potentially achieve your financial goals.

Why Most Traders Lose

Trading, often romanticized as a path to quick riches, is a complex and challenging endeavor. The allure of financial freedom draws countless individuals into the markets, but the reality is harsh: the vast majority of traders end up losing money. This chapter delves into the key reasons behind this phenomenon, providing insights that can help you navigate the treacherous waters of trading and increase your chances of success.

1. Lack of a Solid Trading Plan

One of the most fundamental reasons for trader failure is the absence of a well-defined trading plan. A trading plan is a comprehensive document that outlines your trading goals, risk tolerance, preferred strategies, and money management rules. Without a plan, traders are like ships without rudders, susceptible to impulsive decisions and emotional trading.

A robust trading plan acts as a roadmap, guiding your actions in both winning and losing trades. It helps you stay disciplined, avoid overtrading, and manage risk effectively. Creating a trading plan requires careful consideration and research, but the effort is well worth it.

2. Emotional Trading

Emotions are the nemesis of many traders. Fear, greed, hope, and despair can cloud judgment and lead to irrational decisions. Fear can cause traders to exit profitable trades prematurely, while greed can lead to holding on to losing trades for too long. Hope can prevent traders from cutting losses, and despair can lead to reckless trading in an attempt to recoup losses quickly.

Successful traders understand the importance of emotional control. They develop strategies to manage their emotions, such as taking breaks during periods of high stress or using stop-loss orders to limit losses. By keeping emotions in check, traders can make more objective decisions based on their trading plan.

3. Overtrading

Overtrading, or excessive trading, is another common pitfall. Traders often feel the need to be constantly in the market, believing that more trades translate to more profits. However, the opposite is often true. Frequent trading can lead to increased transaction costs and expose traders to unnecessary risks.

It's essential to be selective and patient in your trading. Focus on high-probability setups that align with your trading plan. Remember, it's better to miss a few trades than to take too many low-quality ones.

4. Poor Risk Management

Risk management is the cornerstone of successful trading. It involves determining how much capital you are willing to risk on each trade and using tools like stop-loss orders to limit potential losses. Many traders neglect risk management, leading to catastrophic losses that can wipe out their accounts.

A common rule of thumb is to risk no more than 1-2% of your trading capital on any single trade. This ensures that even a string of losing trades won't significantly impact your overall account balance. Additionally, it's important to have a clear exit strategy for both winning and losing trades.

5. Chasing Hot Tips and Market Noise

The financial markets are filled with noise – rumors, news headlines, and expert opinions that can influence traders' decisions. Chasing hot tips or reacting to every piece of market news can be detrimental to your trading performance.

It's crucial to develop a filter for information and focus on your trading plan. Don't let external noise distract you from your strategy. Remember, successful trading is about discipline and consistency, not reacting to every market fluctuation.

6. Lack of Education and Continuous Learning

Trading is a dynamic field that requires continuous learning and adaptation. Markets evolve, and new strategies emerge. Traders who fail to keep up with the latest developments risk falling behind and losing their edge.

Invest in your education by reading books, attending webinars, and taking courses from reputable sources. Engage with other traders and learn from their experiences. The more you know, the better equipped you'll be to navigate the complexities of the market.

7. Unrealistic Expectations

Many new traders enter the market with unrealistic expectations of overnight success. They see stories of traders making millions and believe that they can achieve the same results quickly and easily. However, trading is a skill that takes time and effort to master.

It's important to set realistic goals and understand that losses are a part of the game. Focus on consistent improvement and long-term profitability, rather than chasing quick wins.

8. Failure to Adapt

Markets are constantly changing, and what works today may not work tomorrow. Traders who cling to outdated strategies or fail to adapt to new market conditions are likely to struggle.

Be flexible and willing to adjust your approach as needed. Continuously analyze your trades and identify areas for improvement. Embrace change and view it as an opportunity for growth.

9. Lack of Patience

Patience is a virtue in trading. Successful traders understand that profitable opportunities don't come around every day. They wait for high-probability setups that align with their trading plan and avoid impulsive trades driven by impatience.

Develop the discipline to wait for the right moment to enter the market. Don't force trades or chase the market. Remember, the best trades often come to those who wait.

10. Ignoring the Importance of Psychology

Trading psychology plays a crucial role in determining your success or failure. Your mindset, beliefs, and emotional state can significantly impact your trading decisions.

Work on developing a positive and resilient mindset. Learn to manage stress and maintain focus even during periods of market volatility. Consider seeking guidance from a trading coach or psychologist to help you address any psychological barriers that may be hindering your progress.

The Ten Natural Laws of Trading

Trading, like any other discipline, operates on a set of fundamental principles. These principles, or "natural laws," govern the dynamics of the market and influence the outcomes of every trade. Understanding these laws is crucial for any trader who aspires to achieve consistent profitability. In this chapter, we will explore ten such natural laws, demystifying them in a straightforward manner and providing you with actionable insights to navigate the markets effectively.

1. The Law of Supply and Demand

This is perhaps the most fundamental law in trading, and it underpins all market movements. In essence, prices rise when demand exceeds supply and fall when supply outweighs demand. This simple principle has profound implications for traders. It means that to identify profitable trading opportunities, you need to understand the forces of supply and demand at play in the market.

Practical Tip: Learn to identify areas of imbalance between supply and demand. These areas often represent potential turning points in the market.

2. The Law of Cause and Effect

Every market move has a cause, and this cause often leaves behind an identifiable footprint on the price chart. This footprint can be a specific pattern, a break of a key level, or a change in volume. Skilled traders learn to read these footprints and anticipate the likely effects.

Practical Tip: Develop your ability to identify the causes behind market moves. This will help you anticipate future price action and make more informed trading decisions.

3. The Law of Effort vs. Result

This law states that the effort expended in a market move should be commensurate with the result achieved. For example, a large increase in buying volume should ideally lead to a significant price rise. If the price rise is disproportionately small, it could indicate weakness in the market, and a potential reversal could be on the horizon.

Practical Tip: Pay attention to the relationship between effort (volume) and result (price movement). Divergences between the two can provide valuable trading signals.

4. The Law of Polarity

This law highlights the dual nature of market trends. Every trend has an uptrend and a downtrend phase. Understanding this polarity helps traders recognize the potential for trend reversals and adjust their strategies accordingly.

Practical Tip: Always be aware of the current market trend and its potential for reversal. Don't get caught on the wrong side of a trend change.

5. The Law of Rhythm

Markets move in a rhythmic fashion, oscillating between periods of expansion and contraction. These rhythms can be observed on multiple timeframes, from short-term intraday charts to long-term weekly or monthly charts. Recognizing these rhythms helps traders anticipate potential turning points and identify high-probability trading setups.

Practical Tip: Learn to identify the dominant market rhythm on your preferred trading timeframe. This will enable you to time your entries and exits more effectively.

6. The Law of Relativity

This law emphasizes that market movements are relative. A strong uptrend in one market may be considered weak in another. Similarly, a price move that seems significant on a short-term chart might be inconsequential on a longer-term chart. Understanding this relativity helps traders maintain perspective and avoid making impulsive decisions based on isolated price movements.

Practical Tip: Always analyze price movements in the context of the broader market and the relevant timeframe.

7. The Law of Impermanence

This law underscores the ever-changing nature of the markets. No trend lasts forever, and no market condition remains static. Traders who cling to outdated beliefs or strategies are likely to struggle in the long run. Adaptability and a willingness to evolve are key traits of successful traders.

Practical Tip: Embrace the dynamic nature of the markets. Continuously learn and refine your trading strategies to stay ahead of the curve.

8. The Law of Probability

Trading is inherently probabilistic. No trading strategy or system can guarantee 100% success. Even the most skilled traders experience losses. The key is to develop a trading approach that tilts the odds in your favor and manage your risk effectively to ensure long-term profitability.

Practical Tip: Focus on developing a trading edge, even a small one. Over time, a small edge can compound into significant profits.

9. The Law of Patience

Patience is a virtue in trading. Rushing into trades or chasing quick profits often leads to costly mistakes. Successful traders understand the importance of waiting for high-probability setups and exercising discipline in their execution.

Practical Tip: Develop a trading plan and stick to it. Avoid impulsive trades driven by emotions or the fear of missing out.

10. The Law of Self-Mastery

The most important battles in trading are fought within ourselves. Emotions like fear and greed can cloud our judgment and lead to irrational decisions. Successful traders learn to master their emotions and maintain a disciplined approach even in the face of adversity.

Practical Tip: Cultivate emotional intelligence and develop strategies to manage your emotions effectively. This will enable you to make rational trading decisions even under pressure.

Understanding Market Structure

In the world of trading, where prices dance and fortunes are made or lost, understanding market structure is akin to deciphering the hidden language of the charts. It is the bedrock upon which successful price action strategies are built. In this chapter, we embark on a journey to unravel the complexities of market structure, presenting it in a straightforward manner for beginners. By the end, you'll possess a solid grasp of this essential concept, empowering you to make more informed trading decisions.

What is Market Structure?

At its core, market structure refers to the way prices organize themselves on a chart over a given period. It is the visual representation of the ongoing battle between buyers (bulls) and sellers (bears). By analyzing market structure, traders gain insights into the prevailing market sentiment, potential turning points, and areas of support and resistance.

The Building Blocks: Trends and Ranges

Market structure is primarily composed of two fundamental building blocks: trends and ranges.

1. Trends:

A trend signifies a sustained directional movement of price, either upwards (uptrend) or downwards (downtrend). Uptrends are characterized by a series of higher highs and higher lows, while downtrends exhibit lower lows and lower highs. Trends can last for varying durations, from short-term swings to long-term movements spanning months or even years.

2. Ranges (or Consolidation):

A range, also known as consolidation, occurs when price moves sideways within a defined area, lacking a clear directional bias. Ranges are characterized by price bouncing between a support level (the lower boundary) and a resistance level (the upper boundary). They often represent periods of indecision in the market, where buyers and sellers are in relative equilibrium.

The Four Primary Market Structures

While trends and ranges are the basic building blocks, market structure can be further classified into four primary types:

1. Uptrend: As mentioned earlier, an uptrend is marked by a series of higher highs and higher lows. In an uptrend, buyers are in control, propelling prices upward. Traders often look for buying opportunities during pullbacks within an uptrend.

2. Downtrend: Conversely, a downtrend consists of lower lows and lower highs. Sellers dominate in a downtrend, pushing prices lower. Traders may seek short-selling opportunities or wait for a trend reversal before entering long positions.

3. Range (Consolidation): Ranges are characterized by price oscillating between support and resistance levels. During ranges, breakouts (price moving beyond the range boundaries) can signal the start of a new trend. Traders might employ strategies that capitalize on the range-bound price action, such as buying near support and selling near resistance.

4. Trend Reversal: A trend reversal occurs when the prevailing trend changes direction. An uptrend reverses into a downtrend, or vice-versa. Identifying trend reversals is crucial for traders to adapt their strategies and avoid being caught on the wrong side of the market.

Identifying Market Structure: A Step-by-Step Approach

Now that we understand the different types of market structure, let's explore how to identify them on a price chart:

1. Identify the Swing Highs and Swing Lows: Swing highs are the peaks in price action, while swing lows are the troughs. By connecting these swing points, we can start to visualize the underlying structure.

2. Determine the Trend: Look for a series of higher highs and higher lows (uptrend) or lower lows and lower highs (downtrend). If neither pattern is evident, the market is likely in a range.

3. Identify Support and Resistance: In an uptrend, prior swing lows often act as support levels, while prior swing highs can become resistance in a downtrend. In a range, the upper and lower boundaries of the price oscillation define the resistance and support levels, respectively.

4. Observe Breakouts: Pay attention to instances where price breaks out of a range or a trendline. Breakouts can signify a potential shift in market structure and offer trading opportunities.

Applying Market Structure to Trading

Understanding market structure provides traders with valuable insights for making informed trading decisions. Here are some key applications:

1. Trend Trading: Identify the prevailing trend and trade in its direction. Buy in uptrends and sell or short-sell in downtrends.

2. Range Trading: In range-bound markets, buy near support and sell near resistance.

3. Breakout Trading: Enter trades when price breaks out of a range or a trendline, anticipating a new trend to emerge.

4. Risk Management: Use support and resistance levels to set stop-loss orders and protect your capital.

Advanced Concepts in Market Structure

While the basics of market structure are relatively straightforward, there are some advanced concepts that traders can explore to enhance their understanding:

1. Multiple Timeframe Analysis: Analyze market structure on different timeframes to gain a broader perspective. The trend on a higher timeframe can influence the price action on lower timeframes.

2. Market Structure Shifts: Be aware that market structure is dynamic and can change over time. A trend can transition into a range, and a range can eventually break out into a new trend.

3. Order Flow Analysis: For experienced traders, incorporating order flow analysis can provide additional insights into market structure and potential turning points.

The Four Types of Market Structure

Understanding market structure is akin to deciphering the underlying DNA of price movements. It's about identifying the dominant forces at play, recognizing recurring patterns, and anticipating potential shifts. For a trader, this knowledge is not just beneficial - it's essential.

In this chapter, we'll delve into the four primary types of market structure: accumulation, distribution, uptrend, and downtrend. We'll explore their characteristics, how to identify them, and, most importantly, how to leverage this knowledge to make informed trading decisions.

The Foundation: Understanding Trends

Before we explore the four market structures, let's establish a fundamental understanding of trends. A trend, in its simplest form, is the general direction in which the price of an asset is moving. We categorize trends into three types:

Uptrend: This is characterized by a series of higher highs and higher lows. In an uptrend, the overall sentiment is bullish, with buyers in control.
Downtrend: This is the opposite of an uptrend, marked by a series of lower highs and lower lows. In a downtrend, the sentiment is bearish, with sellers dominating the market.
Sideways Trend (Range): In this scenario, the price oscillates between a well-defined support and resistance level, with no clear upward or downward bias.

Now, let's explore how these trends manifest into the four distinct market structures.

1. Accumulation: The Quiet Before the Storm

Imagine a tug-of-war where both teams are equally matched, neither side gaining a clear advantage. This stalemate is akin to the accumulation phase in the market. It's a period where large, institutional players are quietly accumulating an asset, often at discounted prices, in anticipation of a future uptrend.

Characteristics:

Sideways Price Action: The price tends to move within a range, with no clear upward or downward bias.
Increased Volume on Down Moves: While the price may dip, these dips are often accompanied by increased volume, indicating strong buying interest at lower levels.
Spring: A 'spring' is a sharp downward movement that tests the commitment of buyers. It's often followed by a quick recovery, signifying that buyers are indeed in control.

Identifying Accumulation:

Support and Resistance: Identify a clear range where the price is oscillating.
Volume Analysis: Look for increased volume on down moves and decreased volume on up moves.
Springs & Tests: Watch for sharp down moves that are quickly bought up.

Trading Opportunities:

Buy on Dips: The accumulation phase offers excellent opportunities to buy an asset at a discount. Look for buying opportunities near the support level or after a 'spring.'

Breakout Trading: Once the price breaks out of the accumulation range with conviction (often accompanied by a surge in volume), it signals the start of an uptrend. This is an opportune time to enter a long position.

2. Distribution: The Calm Before the Fall

If accumulation is the quiet before the storm, then distribution is the calm before the fall. It's the phase where institutional players, having reaped profits during the uptrend, start to unload their positions.

Characteristics:

Sideways Price Action: Similar to accumulation, the price moves within a range, but with a subtle difference - the overall sentiment is starting to shift.

Decreased Volume on Up Moves: While the price may rally, these rallies are often accompanied by decreased volume, indicating waning buying interest.

Upthrust: An 'upthrust' is a sharp upward movement that traps overeager buyers. It's often followed by a swift reversal, signaling that sellers are now in control.

Identifying Distribution:

Support and Resistance: Identify a range where the price is consolidating, but pay close attention to failed breakouts above the resistance level.
Volume Analysis: Look for decreased volume on up moves and increased volume on down moves.
Upthrusts & Tests: Watch for sharp up moves that are quickly sold into.

Trading Opportunities:

Sell on Rallies: Distribution phases offer good opportunities to sell an asset or initiate short positions. Look for selling opportunities near the resistance level or after an 'upthrust.'
Breakdown Trading: Once the price breaks down from the distribution range with conviction, it signals the start of a downtrend. This is an opportune time to enter a short position.

3. Uptrend: Riding the Wave

An uptrend is the dream scenario for any trader. It's a period of sustained upward momentum, characterized by a series of higher highs and higher lows.

Characteristics:

Higher Highs and Higher Lows: The price consistently makes new highs, and any pullbacks (lows) are higher than the previous ones.

Strong Buying Pressure: Buyers are clearly in control, driving the price higher.

Pullbacks are Shallow: Any dips in price are usually shallow and quickly bought up.

Identifying an Uptrend:

Trendlines: Draw a trendline connecting the lows. In an uptrend, the price should respect this trendline, bouncing off it on pullbacks.

Moving Averages: The price should be trading above its key moving averages (e.g., 50-day, 200-day).

Momentum Indicators: Indicators like the Relative Strength Index (RSI) or Moving Average Convergence Divergence (MACD) should confirm the upward momentum.

Trading Opportunities:

Buy on Dips: The golden rule in an uptrend is to 'buy the dips.' Look for opportunities to enter long positions when the price pulls back to the trendline or key moving averages.

Breakout Trading: In an uptrend, the price often consolidates before making another push higher. Look for breakouts from these consolidation patterns to enter long positions.

4. Downtrend: Navigating the Decline

A downtrend is the flip side of an uptrend. It's a period of sustained downward momentum, marked by a series of lower highs and lower lows.

Characteristics:

Lower Highs and Lower Lows: The price consistently makes new lows, and any rallies (highs) are lower than the previous ones.
Strong Selling Pressure: Sellers are in control, pushing the price lower.
Rallies are Shallow: Any bounces in price are usually shallow and quickly sold into.

Identifying a Downtrend:

Trendlines: Draw a trendline connecting the highs. In a downtrend, the price should respect this trendline, bouncing off it on rallies.
Moving Averages: The price should be trading below its key moving averages.
Momentum Indicators: Indicators like the RSI or MACD should confirm the downward momentum.

Trading Opportunities:

Sell on Rallies: In a downtrend, the strategy is to 'sell the rallies.' Look for opportunities to enter short positions when the price bounces to the trendline or key moving averages.
Breakdown Trading: Similar to uptrends, the price often consolidates before making another push lower in a downtrend. Look for breakdowns from these consolidation patterns to enter short positions.

Putting it all together: Market Structure & Trading

Understanding market structure is not just about identifying trends; it's about understanding the underlying forces that drive them. By recognizing the different phases of the market - accumulation, distribution, uptrend, and downtrend - you can gain a significant edge in your trading.

Remember, the market is dynamic, and these phases are not always clear-cut. However, by developing the skill to identify these structures, you can time your entries and exits more effectively, manage your risk more prudently, and ultimately, increase your chances of becoming a consistently profitable trader.

Key Takeaways:

Market structure provides a framework for understanding the underlying forces driving price movements.
The four primary market structures are accumulation, distribution, uptrend, and downtrend.
Each structure has unique characteristics that can be identified using price action, volume analysis, and technical indicators.
By recognizing these structures, traders can make more informed decisions about when to enter and exit trades.
Market structure analysis is a valuable tool for any trader, regardless of their preferred trading style or time frame.

How to Identify Market Structure

Market structure, in its simplest form, describes the current state of the market. Is it trending upwards (bullish), downwards (bearish), or moving sideways (range-bound)? Understanding market structure is paramount for any trader as it provides a framework to interpret price action and make informed trading decisions. This chapter will delve into the intricacies of market structure, providing beginners with clear, actionable insights.

The Foundation: Uptrends, Downtrends, and Ranges

At its core, market structure is built on three primary states:

1. Uptrend: An uptrend is characterized by a series of higher highs and higher lows. In an uptrend, buyers are in control, consistently pushing prices to new highs.

2. Downtrend: Conversely, a downtrend exhibits lower highs and lower lows. Sellers dominate in a downtrend, driving prices lower.

3. Range (Sideways Trend): A range occurs when prices oscillate between a defined support and resistance level. Neither buyers nor sellers have a clear advantage, leading to a sideways price movement.

Identifying Trends: The Importance of Swing Highs and Swing Lows

The cornerstone of recognizing market structure lies in identifying swing highs and swing lows.

- Swing High: A swing high is a candlestick with a higher high than the candlesticks on both sides of it. It signifies a temporary peak in price before a pullback.
- Swing Low: A swing low is a candlestick with a lower low than the candlesticks on both sides of it. It marks a temporary bottom in price before a bounce.

By connecting these swing highs and swing lows, we can visually represent the prevailing trend:

Uptrend: An uptrend is confirmed when we see a series of higher swing highs and higher swing lows.

Downtrend: A downtrend is established when we observe lower swing highs and lower swing lows.

Range: In a range, swing highs and swing lows tend to stay within a horizontal channel, indicating a lack of directional momentum.

Beyond the Basics: Internal Structure and Fractals

While identifying the primary trend is crucial, experienced traders go a step further by analyzing the internal structure of a trend. This involves recognizing smaller trends (or fractals) within the larger trend.

Uptrend Internal Structure: Within an uptrend, there will be minor pullbacks or consolidations. These pullbacks often form smaller downtrends or ranges, but the overall trajectory remains upward as long as the higher highs and higher lows structure persists.

Downtrend Internal Structure: Similarly, a downtrend will have intermittent bounces or consolidations, which can be identified as smaller uptrends or ranges. The overarching trend remains downward as long as lower highs and lower lows are established.

Understanding these internal structures is vital because they provide potential entry and exit points within the broader trend. For example, in an uptrend, traders might look to buy during a pullback (the minor downtrend within the uptrend) with the expectation that the price will resume its upward movement.

Market Structure Shift: Break of Structure (BOS)

Markets are dynamic, and trends don't last forever. A crucial concept in market structure analysis is the 'Break of Structure' (BOS). A BOS signals a potential change in the prevailing trend.

BOS in an Uptrend: A BOS in an uptrend occurs when the price creates a lower low, breaking the sequence of higher lows. This suggests a potential trend reversal or, at the very least, a significant pullback.

BOS in a Downtrend: In a downtrend, a BOS happens when the price forms a higher high, violating the series of lower highs. This indicates a possible trend reversal or a strong bounce.

Recognizing a BOS allows traders to adapt their strategies. A BOS in an uptrend might prompt traders to take profits or tighten stop losses, while a BOS in a downtrend might signal a potential buying opportunity.

Putting It All Together: A Step-by-Step Guide to Identifying Market Structure

1. Identify Swing Highs and Swing Lows: Mark the swing highs and swing lows on your chart.

2. Connect the Swing Points: Connect the swing highs and swing lows to visualize the trend.

3. Determine the Trend:
   Uptrend: Higher highs and higher lows.
   Downtrend: Lower highs and lower lows.
   Range: Prices oscillate between support and resistance.

4. Analyze the Internal Structure: Look for smaller trends or consolidations within the larger trend.

5. Watch for BOS: Be alert for a break of structure, signaling a potential trend change.

Practical Tips for Beginners

Start with Higher Timeframes: Begin your analysis on higher timeframes (e.g., daily or 4-hour charts) to get a clear picture of the overall trend. Then, you can drill down to lower timeframes for potential entry and exit points.

Use Multiple Confirmations: Don't rely solely on swing highs and swing lows. Look for confluence with other technical tools like trendlines, moving averages, or volume analysis to strengthen your market structure assessment.

Practice and Patience: Identifying market structure takes practice. Start by analyzing historical charts and gradually apply your skills to live markets. Be patient and don't get discouraged if you make mistakes initially.

Keep a Trading Journal: A trading journal is invaluable for tracking your market structure analysis and reviewing your trades. It helps identify areas for improvement and refine your trading strategies.

Using Market Structure to Your Advantage

Market structure is the underlying DNA of any financial market. Like a skilled detective deciphers clues to solve a mystery, a successful trader decodes market structure to anticipate potential price movements and make informed trading decisions. This chapter will delve into the concept of market structure, focusing on its four primary types and how understanding them can empower you to trade with greater precision and profitability.

What is Market Structure?

In essence, market structure refers to the organization and arrangement of price action over a given period. It helps us identify the current market environment – whether it favors buyers (bullish), sellers (bearish), or is in a state of equilibrium (sideways).

The Four Types of Market Structure

1. Accumulation (Uptrend): In an accumulation phase, the market is in an overall uptrend, but with intermittent pullbacks. Buyers are gradually accumulating assets, leading to higher highs and higher lows.

Key Characteristics:

Higher highs and higher lows
Bullish momentum
Pullbacks are shallow and brief
Buying pressure outweighs selling pressure

Trading Opportunities:
Look for buying opportunities during pullbacks
Aim for long (buy) positions
Set stop-loss orders below recent swing lows

2. Distribution (Downtrend): During distribution, the market is in a general downtrend, punctuated by temporary rallies. Sellers are distributing their assets, resulting in lower highs and lower lows.

Key Characteristics:
Lower highs and lower lows
Bearish momentum
Rallies are short-lived
Selling pressure dominates buying pressure

Trading Opportunities:
Seek selling opportunities during rallies
Aim for short (sell) positions
Set stop-loss orders above recent swing highs

3. Range (Sideways Market): In a range or sideways market, prices oscillate between well-defined support

and resistance levels. There is a relative balance between buyers and sellers.

Key Characteristics:
   Prices trade within a horizontal channel
   No clear trend
   Support and resistance levels are respected

Trading Opportunities:
   Buy near support, sell near resistance
   Use range-bound trading strategies
   Be cautious of breakouts

4. Reversal (Change in Trend): Reversals mark a significant shift in market sentiment and direction. An uptrend reverses into a downtrend (or vice versa).

Key Characteristics:
   Breakout from previous market structure
   Change in momentum
   Potential for significant price movement

Trading Opportunities:
   Trade in the direction of the new trend
   Exercise caution, as false breakouts can occur

How to Identify Market Structure

Price Action: Carefully observe the formation of highs and lows. Higher highs and higher lows indicate an uptrend (accumulation), while lower highs and lower lows suggest a downtrend (distribution).

Trendlines: Draw trendlines to connect swing highs and swing lows. An upward sloping trendline confirms an uptrend, a downward sloping trendline indicates a downtrend, and a horizontal trendline reveals a range.

Moving Averages: Moving averages can help identify the prevailing trend. In an uptrend, prices tend to stay above a moving average, while in a downtrend, prices usually stay below it.

Volume: Volume can provide valuable clues about market strength. Increasing volume during an uptrend or downtrend reinforces the trend, whereas decreasing volume may signal a potential reversal.

Using Market Structure to Your Advantage

Trade with the Trend: Identify the prevailing market structure and trade in its direction. Buy in uptrends and sell in downtrends. Avoid fighting the trend.

Identify Key Levels: Locate support and resistance levels. These areas often present opportunities for entries, exits, or setting stop-loss orders.

Anticipate Reversals: Recognize signs of potential reversals, such as breakouts from established market structures, changes in momentum, or candlestick patterns suggesting a shift in sentiment.

Manage Risk: Use stop-loss orders to protect your capital. Set them based on the market structure and your risk tolerance.

Be Patient: Wait for high-probability setups that align with the market structure. Avoid impulsive trades based on emotions or hunches.

Practical Examples

1. Accumulation (Uptrend):   You identify an uptrend in the EUR/USD currency pair with higher highs and higher lows. During a pullback to a support level, you enter a long (buy) position, anticipating the uptrend to continue. You place your stop-loss below the recent swing low.

2. Distribution (Downtrend): You observe a downtrend in the stock market with lower highs and lower lows. During a brief rally to a resistance level, you enter a short (sell) position, expecting the downtrend to resume. Your stop-loss is placed above the recent swing high.

3. Range (Sideways Market): The price of gold is trading within a horizontal channel between $1,800 and $1,900. You buy near the support level of $1,800 and sell near

the resistance level of $1,900, taking advantage of the price oscillations within the range.

4. Reversal (Change in Trend): The price of Bitcoin breaks out above a key resistance level, signaling a potential reversal from a downtrend to an uptrend. You enter a long position, aiming to capitalize on the new bullish momentum.

Understanding and utilizing market structure is a fundamental skill for any trader. By recognizing the four primary types of market structure – accumulation, distribution, range, and reversal – you can gain a significant edge in the markets. Remember to trade with the trend, identify key levels, anticipate reversals, manage risk, and exercise patience. As you become more proficient in analyzing market structure, you'll be well on your way to becoming a consistently profitable trader.

Market structure analysis is just one tool in a trader's toolbox. It should be used in conjunction with other technical and fundamental analysis techniques.
No trading strategy is foolproof. There will always be risks involved. Always manage your risk and protect your capital.

Continuous learning and practice are essential for success in trading. Never stop seeking knowledge and refining your skills.

Additional Tips:

- Start by practicing on a demo account to gain experience without risking real money.
- Keep a trading journal to track your progress and identify areas for improvement.
- Seek guidance from experienced traders or mentors.
- Stay disciplined and avoid emotional trading.

By mastering the art of market structure analysis and combining it with sound risk management principles, you can unlock the potential for consistent profitability in the exciting world of trading.

Mastering Support & Resistance: The Cornerstones of Price Action

In the dynamic world of trading, where prices ebb and flow like the tides, two fundamental concepts stand as unwavering pillars: Support and Resistance. Like invisible barriers on a price chart, they mark the zones where buying and selling pressures clash. Understanding Support & Resistance is akin to learning the language of the market, enabling you to anticipate potential price reversals, breakouts, and optimal entry and exit points.

In this chapter, we'll embark on a journey to unravel the mysteries of Support & Resistance. We will delve into the mechanics of identifying these levels, recognizing the signs of their impending breakouts, and explore effective trading strategies that harness their power. Whether you're a novice or a seasoned trader, mastering Support & Resistance will undoubtedly elevate your trading prowess and pave the way for consistent profitability.

Identifying Support & Resistance Levels

Support and Resistance levels represent price zones where the market has historically shown a tendency to reverse or stall. Support acts as a floor, preventing prices from falling further, while Resistance acts as a ceiling, hindering further upward movement. Identifying these levels requires keen observation and an understanding of market psychology.

1. Horizontal Support & Resistance

The most straightforward form of Support & Resistance is horizontal lines drawn across previous price peaks (Resistance) and troughs (Support). These levels signify areas where buyers and sellers have previously engaged in significant battles, leaving a mark on the price chart.

Multiple Touches: The strength of a Support or Resistance level increases with each subsequent touch. A level that has been tested multiple times indicates a strong confluence of buying or selling interest.
Psychological Levels: Round numbers often act as natural Support & Resistance levels due to their psychological significance. Traders tend to place orders around these levels, creating areas of increased activity.

2. Trendlines

In trending markets, trendlines serve as dynamic Support & Resistance levels. An uptrend line connects a series of higher lows, signifying an upward sloping Support level. Conversely, a downtrend line connects a series of lower highs, representing a downward sloping Resistance level.

Angle of the Trendline: The steeper the angle of the trendline, the less reliable it becomes as Support or Resistance. A shallower angle indicates a more sustainable trend and a stronger level.

3. Moving Averages

Moving averages, particularly the commonly used 50-day and 200-day moving averages, can act as dynamic Support & Resistance levels. In an uptrend, the moving average often provides Support, while in a downtrend, it acts as Resistance.

Crossovers: When the price crosses above a moving average, it can signal a potential bullish breakout, while a cross below may indicate a bearish breakdown.

4. Fibonacci Retracement Levels

Fibonacci retracement levels are derived from the Fibonacci sequence, a mathematical series found in nature. These levels, commonly plotted at 38.2%, 50%, and 61.8%, often coincide with areas of potential Support & Resistance in price retracements within a trend.

When Support & Resistance Breaks

Support & Resistance levels are not impenetrable barriers; they can and do break. A break of Support signifies a shift in market sentiment from bullish to bearish, while a break of Resistance indicates a shift from bearish to bullish. Recognizing the signs of an impending breakout is crucial for traders to capitalize on these opportunities.

1. False Breakouts

A false breakout occurs when the price briefly breaches a Support or Resistance level but fails to sustain the move, quickly reversing back within the previous range. These false signals can trap traders on the wrong side of the market, leading to losses.

Volume Confirmation: A genuine breakout is often accompanied by a surge in trading volume, indicating strong conviction behind the move. A false breakout, on the other hand, typically lacks significant volume.

2. Retest of the Broken Level

After a genuine breakout, the price often retraces back to the broken Support or Resistance level, now acting as the opposite. This retest offers an excellent opportunity for traders to enter the market in the direction of the breakout with a favorable risk-to-reward ratio.

Trading Strategies with Support & Resistance

Support & Resistance levels provide a framework for a plethora of trading strategies, catering to various trading styles and risk appetites. Let's explore a few popular strategies that leverage these levels:

1. Breakout Trading

Breakout trading involves entering the market when the price decisively breaks through a Support or Resistance level. This strategy aims to capture the momentum of a new trend as it emerges.

Buy Stop Orders: Place a buy stop order slightly above a Resistance level to automatically enter a long position upon a breakout.
Sell Stop Orders: Place a sell stop order slightly below a Support level to automatically enter a short position upon a breakdown.

2. Range Trading

Range trading capitalizes on price oscillations within a defined Support & Resistance zone. This strategy is ideal for markets experiencing sideways or consolidating price action.

Buy at Support, Sell at Resistance: Enter long positions near Support and take profits near Resistance. Conversely, enter short positions near Resistance and take profits near Support.

3. Pullback Trading

Pullback trading involves entering the market in the direction of the prevailing trend after a temporary pullback to a Support or Resistance level. This strategy offers a more conservative approach to trend trading.

Wait for Confirmation: Look for candlestick patterns or other technical indicators to confirm the pullback is complete before entering a trade.

4. Support & Resistance Flips

When a Support level is broken, it often transforms into a new Resistance level. Similarly, a broken Resistance level can become a new Support level. These "flips" present trading opportunities as the market re-evaluates the significance of these levels.

Support & Resistance are not merely lines on a chart; they are manifestations of the underlying forces of supply and demand. Mastering the identification and interpretation of these levels empowers traders to navigate the markets with greater confidence and precision. By incorporating Support & Resistance into your trading arsenal, you equip yourself with a powerful tool to identify high-probability trading opportunities and manage risk effectively.

Support & Resistance levels are not foolproof. False breakouts and unexpected market events can occur. Therefore, prudent risk management and a disciplined approach are essential for long-term success in trading. As you continue your trading journey, embrace the dynamic nature of Support & Resistance, refine your skills, and adapt your strategies to the ever-changing market landscape. With dedication and perseverance, you can unlock the true potential of these cornerstone concepts and achieve consistent profitability in your trading endeavors.

The Secret to Reading Candlestick Patterns

Candlestick patterns, often referred to as the "secret language of the markets," are a visual representation of price action over a specific time period. They provide valuable insights into the balance between buyers and sellers, offering clues about potential future price movements. For beginners, mastering candlestick patterns can be a game-changer, opening doors to more informed trading decisions and potentially more profitable outcomes.

The Anatomy of a Candlestick

Before delving into the intricacies of candlestick patterns, let's first break down the basic structure of a single candlestick:

Body: The main rectangular part of the candlestick, representing the price range between the opening and closing prices.

White/Green Body: Indicates that the closing price was higher than the opening price (a bullish candlestick).

Black/Red Body: Indicates that the closing price was lower than the opening price (a bearish candlestick).

Shadows/Wicks: The thin lines extending above and below the body, showing the high and low prices reached during the time period.

Upper Shadow: The distance between the high price and the closing price (or opening price if the candlestick is bearish).

Lower Shadow: The distance between the low price and the opening price (or closing price if the candlestick is bearish).

The Timeframe Matters

Candlesticks can be plotted on various timeframes, ranging from minutes to months. The timeframe you choose will influence the patterns you observe and their potential implications.

Short Timeframes (e.g., 1-minute, 5-minute): Offer a more granular view of price action, suitable for day traders looking for quick opportunities. However, they can also be more prone to "noise" and false signals.

Longer Timeframes (e.g., daily, weekly): Provide a broader perspective on market trends, suitable for swing traders and investors with a longer-term outlook. Patterns on longer timeframes tend to be more reliable but may take longer to develop.

Basic Candlestick Patterns and Their Significance

Let's explore some of the most common candlestick patterns that beginners should familiarize themselves with:

1. Hammer and Hanging Man

Appearance:
    Small body at the upper end of a long lower shadow.
    Can be bullish (white/green) or bearish (black/red).

Significance:
    Hammer: Suggests a potential bullish reversal after a downtrend.
    Hanging Man: Suggests a potential bearish reversal after an uptrend.
        The longer the lower shadow, the stronger the potential reversal signal.

2. Bullish and Bearish Engulfing

Appearance:
    Two candlesticks.
    The second candlestick completely engulfs the body of the first candlestick.

Significance:

Bullish Engulfing: A bullish candlestick engulfs a preceding bearish candlestick, suggesting a potential bullish reversal.

Bearish Engulfing: A bearish candlestick engulfs a preceding bullish candlestick, suggesting a potential bearish reversal.

3. Morning Star and Evening Star

Appearance:

Three candlesticks.

The first candlestick is long (bullish or bearish).

The second candlestick is small with a short body (often a Doji or Spinning Top).

The third candlestick is long in the opposite direction of the first candlestick.

Significance:

Morning Star: Suggests a potential bullish reversal after a downtrend.

Evening Star: Suggests a potential bearish reversal after an uptrend.

4. Doji

Appearance:

The opening and closing prices are very close or the same, resulting in a very small or no body.

Significance:

Indicates indecision in the market.

Can signal a potential reversal or continuation of the current trend, depending on the context and surrounding candlesticks.

5. Spinning Top

Appearance:

Small body with relatively long upper and lower shadows.

Significance:

Indicates indecision or a potential pause in the current trend.

The market is in a state of equilibrium, with neither buyers nor sellers gaining a clear advantage.

The Secret: Context is Key

While candlestick patterns can offer valuable clues about market sentiment, it's crucial to remember that they are most effective when interpreted within the broader context of the market. Consider the following factors when analyzing candlestick patterns:

- Trend: Is the market in an uptrend, downtrend, or sideways trend?
- Support and Resistance: Are there any significant support or resistance levels nearby?
- Volume: Is the volume confirming the pattern?
- Other Indicators: Are other technical indicators supporting the pattern?

Tips for Beginners

- Start with the Basics: Focus on mastering a few key candlestick patterns before moving on to more complex ones.
-
- Practice on Historical Charts: Use historical charts to identify and analyze candlestick patterns in different market conditions.

Combine with Other Tools: Use candlestick patterns in conjunction with other technical analysis tools, such as trend lines, moving averages, and oscillators, to confirm your trading signals.

Manage Your Risk: Always use proper risk management techniques, such as stop-loss orders, to protect your capital.

Be Patient: It takes time and practice to become proficient at reading candlestick patterns. Don't get discouraged if you don't see immediate results.

Candlestick patterns are a powerful tool for technical analysis, offering valuable insights into market sentiment and potential price movements. By mastering the art of reading candlestick patterns, beginners can gain a significant edge in their trading journey. Remember, context is key, and combining candlestick patterns with other technical analysis tools can help you make more informed trading decisions. With dedication, practice, and proper risk management, you can unlock the secrets of the markets and pave the way to profitable trading.

Common Candlestick Patterns

Candlestick patterns are the visual representation of price action over a given period. Each candlestick tells a story about the battle between buyers (bulls) and sellers (bears) during that timeframe. Recognizing these patterns can offer valuable insights into potential future price movements, empowering traders to make more informed decisions. Let's delve into some of the most common and reliable candlestick patterns.

1. The Hammer and the Hanging Man

Appearance:
Both have a small body with a long lower wick, signifying a strong rejection of lower prices.
The hammer appears in a downtrend, suggesting a potential reversal to the upside.
The hanging man appears in an uptrend, hinting at a possible reversal to the downside.

Psychology:
Sellers pushed the price down, but buyers stepped in aggressively, driving the price back up (or near its opening) before the close.
In a downtrend, this indicates waning selling pressure and potential buying interest.
In an uptrend, it shows potential exhaustion among buyers and increasing selling pressure.

Trading Implication:
Hammer: Look for confirmation of a bullish reversal with subsequent price action (e.g., a bullish engulfing pattern or a break above a resistance level).
Hanging Man: Look for confirmation of a bearish reversal with subsequent price action (e.g., a bearish engulfing pattern or a break below a support level).

2. The Engulfing Pattern

Appearance:

Consists of two candlesticks.

The second candle completely engulfs the body of the first candle.

A bullish engulfing pattern has a large green (or white) candle engulfing a smaller red (or black) candle.

A bearish engulfing pattern has a large red (or black) candle engulfing a smaller green (or white) candle.

Psychology:

Bullish Engulfing: Buyers have taken control, overwhelming the sellers.

Bearish Engulfing: Sellers have taken control, overpowering the buyers.

Trading Implication:

Bullish Engulfing: Potential bullish reversal, especially when appearing at the bottom of a downtrend or near a support level.

Bearish Engulfing: Potential bearish reversal, particularly when appearing at the top of an uptrend or near a resistance level.

3. The Doji

Appearance:

A candlestick with virtually no body, indicating that the opening and closing prices are very close or the same.

Can have long or short wicks.

Psychology:

Indecision in the market. Neither buyers nor sellers could gain a clear advantage.

Trading Implication:

Suggests a potential reversal or a continuation of the current trend, depending on the context.

Look for confirmation from subsequent candlesticks or other technical indicators.

4. The Morning Star and the Evening Star

Appearance:

Consist of three candlesticks.

Morning Star: A downtrend, followed by a small-bodied candlestick (can be any color), then a large green (or white) candlestick.

Evening Star: An uptrend, followed by a small-bodied candlestick (can be any color), then a large red (or black) candlestick.

Psychology:

Morning Star: The downtrend is losing momentum, and buyers are starting to take control.

Evening Star: The uptrend is losing steam, and sellers are starting to gain control.

Trading Implication:
Morning Star: Potential bullish reversal.
Evening Star: Potential bearish reversal.

5. Additional Patterns

Three White Soldiers and Three Black Crows: Indicate strong continuation of an uptrend (three white soldiers) or a downtrend (three black crows).
Tweezer Tops and Bottoms: Two candlesticks with matching highs (tweezer tops) or lows (tweezer bottoms), signaling potential reversal points.
Harami: A small candlestick contained within the body of a larger candlestick, suggesting a potential slowdown or reversal.

Important Considerations for Beginners

- Context is Key: Always consider the overall market context when interpreting candlestick patterns. A pattern might have a different meaning depending on its location within a trend or near support and resistance levels.

- Confirmation is Crucial: Don't rely solely on a single candlestick pattern. Look for confirmation from subsequent price action or other technical indicators.
- Practice and Patience: It takes time and practice to master the art of reading candlestick patterns. Start with a few simple patterns and gradually expand your repertoire.

Candlestick patterns are a powerful tool for technical analysis, but they are just one piece of the puzzle. Combine your understanding of candlestick patterns with other technical indicators and a sound risk management strategy to enhance your trading success. Remember, the market is dynamic and ever-changing. Continuous learning and adaptation are essential for navigating its complexities.

Additional Tips:

- Backtest your strategies: Test your candlestick pattern trading strategies on historical data to see how they would have performed in the past. This can help you refine your strategies and avoid costly mistakes.
- Use a demo account: Practice trading with a demo account before risking real money. This

will allow you to get comfortable with the platform and test your strategies in a risk-free environment.

- Keep a trading journal: A trading journal can help you track your progress, identify your strengths and weaknesses, and make adjustments to your trading plan.

Trading involves risk, and there is no guarantee of profit. Always trade with money you can afford to lose, and never invest more than you are comfortable losing.

Disclaimer: The information provided in this chapter is for educational purposes only and should not be considered financial advice. Always do your own research and consult with a financial advisor before making any investment decisions.

Remember: Consistent practice and discipline are the hallmarks of successful traders. With dedication and a willingness to learn, you can leverage candlestick patterns to gain a deeper understanding of the market and improve your trading outcomes.

Using Candlestick Patterns for Entries & Exits

Candlestick patterns are visual representations of price action over a specific period. They provide insights into market sentiment and potential turning points, making them invaluable tools for traders seeking well-timed entries and exits. In this chapter, we'll delve into the fundamentals of candlestick patterns, focusing on how beginners can leverage them to enhance their trading decisions.

Understanding Candlestick Basics

Each candlestick comprises a body and two wicks (also called shadows or tails). The body represents the opening and closing prices, while the wicks indicate the high and low prices during the period. A green (or white) body signifies a bullish candle where the closing price is higher than the opening price. Conversely, a red (or black) body denotes a bearish candle where the closing price is lower than the opening price.

Key Candlestick Patterns for Beginners

Hammer and Hanging Man: These patterns have a small body and a long lower wick, indicating a potential reversal. A hammer occurs in a downtrend and suggests a bullish reversal, while a hanging man forms in an uptrend and hints at a bearish reversal. The long lower wick signifies that buyers stepped in to push the price back up (in the case of a hammer) or sellers entered to drive the price down (in the case of a hanging man).

Engulfing Pattern: This pattern consists of two candles, where the second candle completely engulfs the body of the first candle. A bullish engulfing pattern occurs in a downtrend and signals a potential upward reversal, with the second green candle engulfing the first red candle. A bearish engulfing pattern happens in an uptrend and suggests a potential downward reversal, with the second red candle engulfing the first green candle.

Doji: A doji is a candlestick with a very small body or no body at all, indicating indecision in the market. The opening and closing prices are almost the same, and the wicks can vary in length. A doji can signal a potential reversal or a continuation of the current trend, depending on the context and other technical indicators.

Morning Star and Evening Star: These patterns consist of three candles. A morning star signals a potential bullish reversal in a downtrend. The first candle is a long red candle, followed by a small-bodied candle (either red or green), and then a long green candle. An evening star indicates a potential bearish reversal in an uptrend. The first candle is a long green candle, followed by a small-bodied candle, and then a long red candle.

Using Candlestick Patterns for Entries

Confirmation: It's important to look for confirmation before entering a trade based on a candlestick pattern. Confirmation can come from other technical indicators, such as moving averages or trendlines, or from the subsequent price action. For example, if you see a hammer pattern in a downtrend, wait for the next candle to close above the hammer's high before entering a long position.

Risk Management: Always use proper risk management techniques, such as setting stop-loss orders, to protect your capital. Place your stop-loss below the low of the candlestick pattern (for long trades) or above the high of the pattern (for short trades).

Context: Consider the overall market context and trend when interpreting candlestick patterns. A pattern that appears in a strong uptrend might have a different meaning than the same pattern that appears in a downtrend or a sideways market.

Using Candlestick Patterns for Exits

Profit Targets: Use candlestick patterns to identify potential profit-taking levels. For example, if you're in a long trade and see a bearish engulfing pattern, consider taking some or all of your profits.

Trailing Stops: Use trailing stops to lock in profits as the price moves in your favor. A trailing stop is a stop-loss order that moves up (for long trades) or down (for short trades) as the price advances, ensuring that you capture a portion of the gains even if the price reverses.

Pattern Failure: Be aware that candlestick patterns can fail to predict future price movements. If a pattern fails to materialize as expected, consider exiting the trade or adjusting your stop-loss.

Additional Tips for Beginners

Focus on a Few Patterns: Start by focusing on a few key candlestick patterns and mastering their identification and interpretation. As you gain experience, you can gradually expand your repertoire of patterns.

Practice on a Demo Account: Practice trading with candlestick patterns on a demo account before risking real money. This will allow you to test your strategies and refine your skills without incurring any financial losses.

Combine with Other Indicators: Candlestick patterns are most effective when used in conjunction with other technical indicators and analysis techniques. Use a combination of tools to confirm your trading decisions and increase your chances of success.

Be Patient and Disciplined: Successful trading requires patience and discipline. Don't rush into trades based on a single candlestick pattern. Wait for confirmation and follow your trading plan.

Candlestick patterns offer valuable insights into market sentiment and potential turning points, making them essential tools for traders of all levels. By understanding the basics of candlestick patterns and applying them in conjunction with other technical analysis techniques, beginners can enhance their trading decisions and increase their chances of success in the financial markets. Remember, practice, patience, and discipline are key to mastering the art of candlestick pattern trading.

MAEE Formula

Applying the MAEE Formula in Bull & Bear Markets

Navigating the financial markets can feel like deciphering an intricate code. Indicators flash, news headlines blare, and charts zigzag, leaving traders overwhelmed and unsure of their next move. Enter the MAEE Formula—a beacon of simplicity in a sea of complexity. It's a trading strategy designed to help you cut through the noise and identify high-probability setups, regardless of whether the market is charging upwards or tumbling downwards.

MAEE stands for:

M - Multiple Timeframe Analysis
A - Area of Value
E - Entry Trigger
E - Exit Strategy

This formula isn't a magic bullet, but rather a structured approach that combines key elements of price action trading to increase your chances of success. By integrating multiple timeframes, identifying key areas where price tends to react, waiting for a precise entry trigger, and having a clear exit plan, you empower yourself to trade with confidence and clarity.

The Core Principles of the MAEE Formula

1. Multiple Timeframe Analysis (M): Just as a skilled sailor uses both a wide-angle view of the horizon and a detailed nautical chart, a successful trader utilizes multiple timeframes to gain a comprehensive understanding of market dynamics. By analyzing the higher timeframe (e.g., daily or weekly) you can identify the overarching trend and potential areas of support and resistance. The lower timeframe (e.g., 15-minute or hourly) allows you to pinpoint precise entry and exit points.

2. Area of Value (A): These are zones on your chart where price has historically shown a tendency to reverse or stall. It could be a previous swing high or low, a trendline, or a significant moving average. Identifying these areas beforehand allows you to anticipate potential turning points and plan your trades accordingly.

3. Entry Trigger (E): This is the specific signal that confirms your trade idea and prompts you to enter the market. It could be a candlestick pattern, a breakout from a consolidation zone, or a confluence of multiple factors.

The entry trigger acts as your green light, ensuring you don't jump the gun or miss the boat.

4. Exit Strategy (E): Before you even enter a trade, you need a clear plan for when to take profits and when to cut losses. This helps manage risk and protect your capital. Your exit strategy might involve trailing stops, profit targets based on support and resistance levels, or a time-based exit.

Applying the MAEE Formula in Bull & Bear Markets

Bull Markets

Multiple Timeframe Analysis:
   Higher Timeframe: Identify an uptrend with higher highs and higher lows.
   Lower Timeframe: Look for pullbacks within the uptrend towards areas of value.

Area of Value:
   Focus on previous swing lows, rising trendlines, or key moving averages that could act as support.

Entry Trigger:

Look for bullish candlestick patterns, breakouts from consolidation zones, or a bullish confluence near the area of value.

Exit Strategy:

Consider trailing stops to lock in profits as the price moves in your favor.

Set profit targets at potential resistance levels or based on a risk-reward ratio.

Bear Markets

Multiple Timeframe Analysis:

Higher Timeframe: Identify a downtrend with lower highs and lower lows.

Lower Timeframe: Look for bounces within the downtrend towards areas of value.

Area of Value:

Focus on previous swing highs, falling trendlines, or key moving averages that could act as resistance.

Entry Trigger:

Look for bearish candlestick patterns, breakouts from consolidation zones, or a bearish confluence near the area of value.

Exit Strategy:

Consider trailing stops to protect your capital as the price moves against you.

Set profit targets at potential support levels or based on a risk-reward ratio.

Examples of MAEE Formula Trades

Examples of MAEE Formula Trades

Example 1: Bullish Trade on EUR/USD (Hourly Chart)

Multiple Timeframe Analysis:
Daily chart shows a clear uptrend.
Hourly chart shows a pullback towards the 50-period moving average (area of value).

Area of Value:
The 50-period moving average is acting as dynamic support.

Entry Trigger:
Bullish engulfing candlestick pattern forms near the 50-period moving average.

Exit Strategy:
Place a stop loss below the recent swing low.

Set a profit target at the previous swing high or based on a 1:2 risk-reward ratio.

Example 2: Bearish Trade on GBP/JPY (15-Minute Chart)

Multiple Timeframe Analysis:
    Hourly chart shows a clear downtrend.
    15-minute chart shows a bounce towards a falling trendline (area of value).

Area of Value:
    The falling trendline is acting as dynamic resistance.

Entry Trigger:
    Bearish pin bar candlestick pattern forms near the falling trendline.

Exit Strategy:
    Place a stop loss above the recent swing high.
    Set a profit target at the previous swing low or based on a 1:2 risk-reward ratio.

Remember: Trading is a Journey, Not a Destination

The MAEE Formula is a powerful tool, but it's not foolproof. No trading strategy guarantees profits on every trade. Market conditions change, and there will be times when your trades don't work out. The key is to stay disciplined, manage your risk, and continuously refine your skills.

As a beginner, start by practicing the MAEE Formula on a demo account. Focus on understanding the core principles and identifying high-probability setups. Don't get discouraged by losses—they are a natural part of the learning process. With patience, persistence, and the MAEE Formula as your guide, you'll be well on your way to becoming a consistently profitable trader.

Tips for Beginners:

- Start small: Don't risk more than you can afford to lose.
- Keep a trading journal: Track your trades, analyze your results, and learn from your mistakes.
- Be patient: Don't expect to become a millionaire overnight. Trading takes time and effort.
- Never stop learning: The markets are constantly evolving, so you need to stay up-to-date with the latest trends and strategies.
- Find a mentor: A mentor can provide valuable guidance and support as you navigate your trading journey.

93

Remember, the MAEE Formula is not just a set of rules; it's a mindset. It's about approaching the market with a structured and disciplined approach. With dedication and practice, you can master this formula and unlock the path to consistent profitability in the exciting world of trading.

Identifying Big Market Moves

In the world of trading, capturing those elusive big market moves can be the difference between average returns and extraordinary profits. These explosive price swings, often driven by significant news events, shifts in market sentiment, or technical breakouts, present unique opportunities for traders who can identify and capitalize on them. But how do you spot the signs of an impending big move before it's too late? In this chapter, we'll delve into the subtle signals and patterns that often precede major market shifts, empowering you to position yourself for potentially significant gains.

Understanding Market Volatility

Before we dive into specific signals, let's establish a foundational understanding of market volatility. Volatility, simply put, is the degree of price fluctuation in a market. High volatility means prices are changing rapidly and dramatically, while low volatility indicates more stable and predictable price action.

Big market moves are often associated with periods of heightened volatility. When volatility spikes, it signals increased market activity and the potential for significant price swings in either direction. Therefore, recognizing changes in volatility is crucial in anticipating potential big moves.

The Signal of Compression

One of the most reliable signals of an impending big move is a phenomenon known as compression. Compression occurs when price action becomes increasingly tight and constricted, with price ranges narrowing and volatility subsiding. This period of relative calm often precedes a significant breakout or breakdown, as market participants build up positions in anticipation of a move.

Think of compression like a coiled spring. The tighter the spring is wound, the more potential energy it stores, and the more forceful its release will be. Similarly, the more compressed price action becomes, the greater the likelihood of a powerful move once the market breaks out of its constrained range.

Identifying Compression

Compression can manifest in several ways on a price chart:

- Narrowing Price Ranges: Observe if the daily or weekly price ranges are shrinking over time. This indicates decreasing volatility and potential compression.

- Tightening Bollinger Bands: Bollinger Bands are a popular volatility indicator that plot standard deviations around a moving average. When the bands contract, it signals decreasing volatility and potential compression.

- Decreasing Average True Range (ATR): ATR measures the average range of price movement over a specified period. A declining ATR suggests decreasing volatility and potential compression.

Triangle Patterns: Triangle patterns, such as symmetrical triangles, ascending triangles, and descending triangles, are classic chart patterns that often signal compression and an impending breakout.

Other Signals of Impending Big Moves

While compression is a key signal, other indicators can also help identify potential big market moves:

- Volume: Volume measures the amount of trading activity in a market. Increasing volume during a period of compression can suggest building market interest and potential for a significant move.

- Breakouts from Key Levels: Breakouts from significant support or resistance levels, trendlines, or chart patterns can trigger powerful moves. Pay close attention to price action around these critical levels.

- News and Events: Major news events, economic data releases, or geopolitical developments can spark significant market volatility and big moves. Stay informed about relevant news and events that could impact your markets.

- Sentiment Extremes: When market sentiment becomes overly bullish or bearish, it can create conditions for a sharp reversal or correction. Monitor sentiment indicators and be cautious when sentiment reaches extreme levels.

Trading Big Market Moves

Once you've identified a potential big move, it's important to develop a sound trading strategy to capitalize on it. Here are some tips:

- Patience: Wait for confirmation of the move before entering a trade. Avoid jumping the gun based on anticipation alone.

- Risk Management: Use appropriate position sizing and stop-loss orders to protect your capital in case the move goes against you.

- Profit Targets: Set realistic profit targets based on the potential size of the move and your risk tolerance.

- Trailing Stops: Consider using trailing stops to lock in profits as the move progresses.

- Flexibility: Be prepared to adjust your strategy as the market evolves. Don't be afraid to take profits or cut losses if necessary.

Example: Identifying and Trading a Big Move

Let's say you're analyzing the EUR/USD currency pair and notice the following:

1. Price has been consolidating in a tight range for several days.
2. Bollinger Bands are contracting, indicating decreasing volatility.
3. ATR is declining.
4. Volume is increasing within the consolidation range.

These signals suggest potential compression and an impending big move. You decide to wait for a breakout from the consolidation range before entering a trade.

The next day, the EUR/USD breaks decisively above the consolidation range on strong volume. You enter a long position with a stop-loss order below the breakout point. The price continues to rally, and you trail your stop-loss to lock in profits. Eventually, you exit the trade with a significant gain as the move starts to lose momentum..

Remember, this is just an example, and real-world trading scenarios can be more complex. It's essential to conduct thorough research and analysis before making any trading decisions.

Additional Tips

Backtesting: Backtest your trading strategies on historical data to assess their effectiveness and identify potential areas for improvement.

Paper Trading: Practice your strategies in a simulated trading environment before risking real capital.

Continuous Learning: Stay updated on market trends, economic developments, and trading techniques through books, courses, and webinars.

Discipline: Stick to your trading plan and avoid impulsive decisions driven by emotions or fear of missing out.

How to Trade Big Market Moves

Big market moves, often referred to as 'breakouts' or 'trends,' are the holy grail for many traders. These significant price surges offer the potential for substantial profits, but they also come with their own set of challenges and risks. For beginners, navigating these powerful market events can be daunting. This subchapter will provide a straightforward guide on how to trade big market moves, emphasizing key concepts and strategies to help you capitalize on these opportunities while managing risks effectively.

Understanding Big Market Moves

A big market move is a sustained and significant price movement in a particular direction. It typically represents a shift in market sentiment or a reaction to a major news event. These moves can last from a few hours to several days or even weeks. They are characterized by increased trading volume and volatility, making them attractive to traders seeking quick profits. However, it's important to recognize that big moves can also reverse sharply, leading to substantial losses if not managed properly.

Key Principles for Trading Big Market Moves

1. Identify the Trend: The first step in trading big moves is to identify the prevailing trend. This can be done using various technical analysis tools, such as trend lines, moving averages, and momentum indicators. The goal is to determine whether the market is in an uptrend, downtrend, or ranging.

2. Wait for Confirmation: Once you've identified a potential trend, wait for confirmation before entering a trade. This can be done by looking for a breakout from a key resistance level (in an uptrend) or a support level (in

a downtrend). A breakout is a strong indication that the market is ready to make a significant move.

3. Use Appropriate Entry Strategies: There are several effective entry strategies for trading big moves, including:

- Breakout Trading: This involves entering a trade when the price breaks out of a key level, such as a resistance or support level, or a trend line. The idea is to catch the move early and ride it as far as possible.

- Pullback Trading: This involves waiting for a pullback (a temporary price retracement) after a breakout before entering a trade. This can help you enter at a better price and reduce your risk.

- Retest Trading: This involves waiting for the price to retest a broken level (resistance turned support or vice versa) before entering a trade. This provides further confirmation of the breakout and can offer a lower-risk entry point.

4. Set Stop-Loss Orders: Stop-loss orders are essential for managing risk in any trade, especially when trading big moves. A stop-loss order is an instruction to automatically close your trade if the price moves against

you by a certain amount. This helps limit your losses and protect your capital.

5. Use Trailing Stop-Loss Orders: Trailing stop-loss orders are a dynamic form of stop-loss that automatically adjusts as the price moves in your favor. This helps you lock in profits and protect your gains as the trend progresses.

6. Manage Your Position Size: Position sizing is crucial for managing risk and preserving your capital. It involves determining the appropriate amount of capital to allocate to each trade based on your risk tolerance and the volatility of the market. A common rule of thumb is to risk no more than 1-2% of your trading capital on any single trade.

7. Be Patient and Disciplined: Trading big moves requires patience and discipline. It's important to wait for the right opportunities and avoid chasing the market. Stick to your trading plan and avoid making impulsive decisions based on emotions or fear of missing out (FOMO).

Illustrative Example: Trading a Breakout

Let's say you've identified an uptrend in a particular stock. You've noticed that the price has been consolidating near a key resistance level for several days. You decide to wait for a breakout above this level before entering a long (buy) trade.

Once the price breaks out above the resistance level with strong volume, you enter a long trade. You set a stop-loss order just below the breakout level to limit your risk. As the price continues to move higher, you adjust your trailing stop-loss to lock in profits.

If the price reverses and hits your stop-loss, you exit the trade with a small loss. However, if the trend continues, you can potentially capture a significant portion of the move and achieve a profitable trade.

Additional Tips for Beginners

- Start Small: When you're first starting out, it's best to trade with a small amount of capital and focus on learning the ropes. As you gain experience and confidence, you can gradually increase your position size.

- Use a Demo Account: A demo account allows you to practice trading with virtual money in a risk-free environment. This is a great way to test your strategies and get comfortable with the trading platform before risking real capital.

- Keep a Trading Journal: A trading journal is a valuable tool for tracking your trades, analyzing your performance, and identifying areas for improvement. It can help you develop discipline and make more informed trading decisions.

- Learn from Experienced Traders: There are many resources available to help you learn from experienced traders, including books, online courses, and trading communities. Take advantage of these resources to expand your knowledge and improve your skills.

- Stay Informed: Stay up-to-date on market news and events that could impact your trades. This includes economic data releases, company earnings reports, and geopolitical developments.

Trading big market moves can be a rewarding but challenging endeavor, especially for beginners. By understanding the key principles, using appropriate strategies, and managing risk effectively, you can increase your chances of success. Remember, patience, discipline, and continuous learning are essential for long-term profitability in the exciting world of trading.

Additional Considerations

- Risk Management: Always prioritize risk management. Never risk more than you can afford to lose on any single trade.

- Emotional Control: Trading can be an emotional rollercoaster. It's important to maintain composure and avoid making impulsive decisions based on fear or greed.

- Continuous Learning: The markets are constantly evolving. Stay curious, keep learning, and adapt your strategies as needed.

Case Studies of Big Market Moves

For a beginner trader, understanding big market moves might feel like trying to decipher a secret code. But these significant shifts in price are not random; they leave clues in their wake. By studying past examples, we can learn to spot the signs and potentially profit from them. Let's delve into a few case studies, breaking them down step-by-step.

Case Study 1: The Brexit Flash Crash

On October 7, 2016, the British pound experienced a sudden and dramatic drop against the US dollar, plunging over 6% in a matter of minutes. This event, known as the "Brexit Flash Crash," was triggered by a combination of factors, including thin liquidity during Asian trading hours, algorithmic trading, and concerns about the UK's exit from the European Union.

The Signal: The pound had been in a downtrend leading up to the crash, reflecting the uncertainty surrounding Brexit. However, the flash crash itself was marked by a sudden, sharp spike in volatility.

The Aftermath: The pound recovered some of its losses, but the event highlighted the risks associated with major political and economic events. Traders who were short the pound during the crash profited handsomely, while those who were long suffered significant losses.

Lessons for Beginners:

- Volatility is your friend (and sometimes your foe): Big moves often come with increased volatility. This can create opportunities for profit, but it also increases risk.
- Stay informed about major news events: Political and economic developments can have a significant impact on the markets.

- Use stop-loss orders: These can help limit your losses if the market moves against you.

Case Study 2: The GameStop Short Squeeze

In early 2021, shares of video game retailer GameStop skyrocketed, driven by a coordinated effort by retail investors on social media platforms like Reddit. This "short squeeze" caught many hedge funds off guard, forcing them to cover their short positions at a massive loss.

The Signal: The initial surge in GameStop's share price was accompanied by a massive increase in trading volume and social media chatter. This suggested that something unusual was happening.

The Aftermath: GameStop's share price eventually pulled back, but the event demonstrated the power of retail investors and the potential risks of short selling.

Lessons for Beginners:

- Don't underestimate the power of social media: Sentiment on social media can drive significant market moves, especially in highly speculative stocks.

- Be cautious with short selling: Short selling can be a profitable strategy, but it also carries significant risk, especially in volatile markets.
- Diversify your portfolio: Don't put all your eggs in one basket. A diversified portfolio can help protect you from unexpected market events.

Case Study 3: The COVID-19 Market Crash

In early 2020, the global stock markets plunged as the COVID-19 pandemic spread around the world. This crash was driven by fears about the economic impact of the virus and the lockdowns that were implemented to contain it.

The Signal: The initial decline in the markets was accompanied by a sharp increase in volatility and a flight to safe-haven assets like gold and US Treasuries.

The Aftermath: The markets eventually recovered, fueled by massive government stimulus and optimism about the development of vaccines. However, the crash served as a reminder of the inherent risks in the markets.

Lessons for Beginners:

- Market crashes are inevitable: Even the most seasoned traders can't predict when a crash will occur.

- Have a plan for dealing with market downturns: This might include reducing your exposure to risky assets, increasing your cash holdings, or even buying the dip if you have a long-term investment horizon.
- Don't panic sell: Selling into a panic can lock in losses and prevent you from participating in the eventual recovery.

Analyzing Big Market Moves: Key Takeaways for Beginners

- Look for changes in volatility: A sudden increase in volatility can be a sign that a big move is underway.
- Pay attention to trading volume: A surge in trading volume can also indicate increased market activity and potential big moves.
- Monitor news and social media: Stay informed about major news events and sentiment on social media.
- Use technical analysis: Technical indicators can help you identify potential support and resistance levels, as well as trend reversals.
- Manage your risk: Use stop-loss orders and position sizing to limit your potential losses.

In-Depth Analysis of a Big Market Move: The 2008 Financial Crisis

To truly grasp the dynamics of a big market move, let's dissect one of the most significant events in recent history: the 2008 financial crisis. This crisis, triggered by the collapse of the US housing market and the subsequent credit crunch, led to a global recession and a sharp decline in stock markets worldwide.

The Lead-Up:

Several factors contributed to the buildup of the crisis:

- Easy credit: Low interest rates and lax lending standards fueled a housing bubble.
- Complex financial instruments: The creation of complex mortgage-backed securities obscured the true risks in the housing market.
- Excessive leverage: Financial institutions took on excessive levels of debt, amplifying their losses when the housing market collapsed.

The Trigger:

The collapse of Lehman Brothers in September 2008 marked a turning point in the crisis. This event triggered a widespread panic in the financial markets, leading to a credit freeze and a sharp decline in economic activity.

The Market Reaction:

The stock markets plunged, with the S&P 500 losing over 50% of its value from its peak in 2007. Volatility soared, and investors fled to safe-haven assets.

The Aftermath:

The crisis led to a global recession, with millions of job losses and widespread economic hardship. Governments and central banks around the world intervened with massive stimulus programs to stabilize the financial system and prevent a complete economic collapse.

Lessons from the 2008 Crisis

- Risk management is paramount: The crisis highlighted the importance of risk management and the dangers of excessive leverage.
- Diversification is key: A diversified portfolio can help mitigate losses during market downturns.
- Stay informed: Understanding the underlying economic and financial conditions can help you anticipate potential risks and opportunities.

- Don't panic: Even in the midst of a crisis, it's important to stay calm and make rational decisions.

Additional Tips for Beginners

Start small: Don't risk more than you can afford to lose.

- Be patient: Profitable trading takes time and discipline.
- Learn from your mistakes: Every trade, whether profitable or not, is a learning opportunity.
- Find a mentor or trading community: Connecting with other traders can provide valuable support and insights.
- Never stop learning: The markets are constantly evolving, so it's important to stay up-to-date on the latest trends and strategies.

Big market moves can be intimidating, but they also present opportunities for profit. By studying past examples, understanding the underlying factors that drive these moves, and implementing sound risk management strategies, you can increase your chances of success in the markets. Remember, trading is a journey, not a destination. With dedication, discipline, and a willingness to learn, you can navigate the complexities of the market and achieve your financial goals.

Advanced Price Action Techniques

In this chapter, we delve deeper into the world of price action, exploring advanced techniques that can significantly enhance your trading prowess. These techniques build upon the foundational knowledge you've acquired, allowing you to refine your entries and exits, manage risk effectively, and adapt to evolving market conditions.

Multi-Timeframe Analysis

- Multi-timeframe analysis is a cornerstone of advanced price action trading. It involves studying price action across multiple timeframes to gain a comprehensive understanding of market trends and identify potential trading opportunities.
- Higher Timeframe Context: The higher timeframe provides the broader context for price action on the lower timeframe. It helps identify the prevailing trend, key support and resistance levels, and potential areas of confluence.
- Lower Timeframe Execution: The lower timeframe is used to fine-tune entries and exits,

identify specific price action patterns, and manage trades more actively.

Example: A trader might use a daily chart to identify the overall trend and key levels, then switch to a 15-minute chart to pinpoint precise entry and exit points based on specific price action patterns.

Price Action and Volume

Volume provides valuable insights into the strength and conviction behind price movements. By analyzing price action in conjunction with volume, traders can gauge the underlying buying or selling pressure and make more informed trading decisions.

- High Volume Breakouts: A breakout accompanied by high volume suggests strong participation and increases the likelihood of a sustained move.
- Low Volume Pullbacks: A pullback with low volume indicates weak selling pressure and may present a buying opportunity.
- Volume Spikes: A sudden spike in volume can signal a potential reversal or the start of a significant trend.

Price Action and Order Flow

Order flow analysis involves studying the actual buy and sell orders placed in the market to gain insights into the underlying supply and demand dynamics. It can help traders anticipate potential price movements and identify favorable trading opportunities.

- Aggression: Order flow analysis can reveal the level of aggression from buyers and sellers, providing clues about potential price direction.
- Absorption: When large orders are absorbed without significant price movement, it suggests strong underlying support or resistance.
- Exhaustion: A decrease in order flow aggression or a shift in the balance of buyers and sellers can signal potential exhaustion and a possible reversal.

Price Action and Market Profile

Market Profile is a graphical representation of price and volume distribution over a specified period. It provides insights into where the majority of trading activity has occurred and can help traders identify key support and resistance levels, potential areas of value, and potential trading opportunities.

- Value Area: The value area represents the price range where the majority of trading activity has occurred. It is often seen as a fair value zone for the underlying asset.

- Point of Control: The point of control is the price level with the highest volume within the value area. It is often seen as a key reference point for traders.
- Profile Shape: The shape of the Market Profile can provide clues about market sentiment and potential future price action.

Price Action and Fibonacci Levels

Fibonacci levels are derived from the Fibonacci sequence, a mathematical sequence found in nature. These levels are often used by traders to identify potential support and resistance levels, set profit targets, and manage risk.

- Key Fibonacci Levels: The key Fibonacci retracement levels are 38.2%, 50%, and 61.8%. These levels are often seen as potential areas where price may reverse or consolidate.
- Fibonacci Extensions: Fibonacci extensions can be used to project potential price targets for continuation moves.
- Fibonacci Fan: The Fibonacci fan can be used to identify potential trendlines and support/resistance levels.

Price Action and Elliott Wave Theory

Elliott Wave Theory is a complex approach to market analysis that suggests price moves in a series of waves. It can be used to identify potential trend patterns, anticipate reversals, and set profit targets.

- Wave Structure: Elliott Wave Theory suggests that price moves in a five-wave impulse pattern followed by a three-wave corrective pattern.
- Wave Degrees: Elliott Wave patterns can be identified across multiple timeframes, from small intraday moves to long-term trends.
- Wave Relationships: The relationships between different waves can provide clues about potential future price action.

Price Action and Wyckoff Method

The Wyckoff Method is a comprehensive approach to market analysis that focuses on identifying accumulation and distribution phases within a trading range. It can be used to anticipate breakouts, identify potential reversals, and manage trades effectively.

- Accumulation: Accumulation is a phase where large players are buying the underlying asset, often at discounted prices.
- Distribution: Distribution is a phase where large players are selling the underlying asset, often at premium prices.
- Wyckoff Schematics: Wyckoff schematics are graphical representations of accumulation and distribution phases, providing insights into potential price action.

Price Action and Harmonic Patterns

Harmonic patterns are geometric price patterns that are based on Fibonacci ratios. They can be used to identify potential reversals, set profit targets, and manage risk.

- Common Harmonic Patterns: Some common harmonic patterns include the Gartley pattern, the Butterfly pattern, and the Bat pattern.
- Pattern Completion: Harmonic patterns are considered complete when price reaches a specific Fibonacci level within the pattern.
- Potential Reversals: Harmonic patterns can signal potential reversals in price action, providing opportunities for traders to enter or exit trades.

Advanced price action techniques offer a powerful toolkit for traders looking to elevate their trading performance. By mastering these techniques, you can gain a deeper understanding of market dynamics, identify high-probability trading opportunities, and manage risk effectively. Remember, consistent practice and continuous learning are essential for achieving long-term success in trading.

As a final word of advice, remember that no single technique or indicator guarantees success in trading. It is important to develop a well-rounded approach that combines multiple tools and techniques, and to always adapt your strategies to changing market conditions. With dedication, discipline, and a commitment to continuous learning, you can achieve your goals and become a consistently profitable trader.

Applying Price Action Across Markets

Forex Trading with Price Action

Forex, or foreign exchange, is the largest and most liquid market in the world, making it an attractive arena for price action traders. The 24-hour nature of the forex market and the abundance of currency pairs provide ample opportunities to apply price action principles. However, forex trading also presents unique challenges due to its volatility and the influence of macroeconomic factors. Let's delve deeper into how to effectively apply price action in the forex market.

Understanding the Forex Market Dynamics

The forex market is driven by a multitude of factors, including economic indicators, central bank policies, geopolitical events, and market sentiment. These factors create a complex and dynamic environment where price action can be influenced by both technical and fundamental forces. To successfully trade forex using price action, it's essential to have a solid understanding of these market dynamics.

- Economic Indicators: Economic indicators such as GDP growth, employment data, inflation rates, and retail sales can significantly impact currency values. Price action traders need to be aware of the release schedule of major economic indicators and how they might affect the currency pairs they are trading.
- Central Bank Policies: Central banks play a crucial role in influencing currency values through interest rate decisions, quantitative easing programs, and other monetary policy tools. Price action traders should closely monitor central bank announcements and speeches to anticipate potential market moves.
- Geopolitical Events: Political events such as elections, wars, and natural disasters can create significant volatility in the forex market. Price action traders need to be aware of the potential impact of geopolitical events and adjust their trading strategies accordingly.
- Market Sentiment: Market sentiment, or the overall mood of traders, can also influence price action. Sentiment can be driven by news headlines, social media trends, and other factors. Price action traders can use sentiment analysis tools to gauge market sentiment and identify potential trading opportunities.

Applying Price Action Concepts to Forex Trading

Once you have a good understanding of the forex market dynamics, you can start applying price action concepts to your trading.

- Identifying Trends: Trend identification is a fundamental aspect of price action trading in any market, including forex. In forex, traders often use multiple timeframes to identify trends. For example, they might use a daily chart to identify the overall trend and a 4-hour chart to identify potential entry and exit points.
- Support and Resistance: Support and resistance levels are crucial in forex trading as they can provide insights into potential price reversals or breakouts. Traders can use price action patterns such as double tops and bottoms, head and shoulders patterns, and trendlines to identify key support and resistance levels.
- Candlestick Patterns: Candlestick patterns are visual representations of price action that can provide valuable information about market sentiment and potential trend reversals. Some common candlestick patterns used in forex trading include engulfing patterns, doji candles, and hammer candles.

- Chart Patterns: Chart patterns such as triangles, flags, and pennants can also be used to identify potential breakouts or trend continuations in the forex market. Traders can use these patterns in conjunction with other price action tools to confirm their trading signals.

Specific Forex Price Action Strategies

- **Pin Bar Trading**: Pin bars are candlestick patterns with long wicks and small bodies that often signal potential trend reversals. Forex traders can use pin bars to identify entry points for trades against the prevailing trend.
- **Inside Bar Trading**: Inside bars are candlestick patterns where the entire candle is contained within the range of the previous candle. Inside bars often signal a period of consolidation before a potential breakout. Forex traders can use inside bars to identify potential breakouts in the direction of the prevailing trend.
- **Breakout Trading**: Breakout trading involves entering a trade when the price breaks out of a key support or resistance level. Forex traders can use price action patterns and chart patterns to identify potential breakout points.
- **Trend Following**: Trend following is a strategy that involves entering trades in the direction of

the prevailing trend. Forex traders can use trendlines, moving averages, and other technical indicators to identify trends and potential entry points.

Risk Management in Forex Price Action Trading

Risk management is crucial in any trading strategy, and forex trading is no exception. Due to the volatility of the forex market, it's essential to have a well-defined risk management plan in place.

- **Position Sizing:** Position sizing refers to the amount of capital you allocate to each trade. It's important to determine your position size based on your risk tolerance and the volatility of the currency pair you are trading.
- **Stop-Loss Orders**: Stop-loss orders are used to limit your losses if the market moves against you. It's essential to place stop-loss orders at a level that allows you to manage your risk while still giving your trade room to breathe.
- **Take-Profit Orders**: Take-profit orders are used to lock in profits when the market moves in your favor. It's important to set realistic take-profit targets based on your trading strategy and the market conditions.

Additional Tips for Forex Price Action Trading

- **Focus on Major Currency Pairs**: Major currency pairs such as EUR/USD, GBP/USD, and USD/JPY tend to be more liquid and less volatile than minor or exotic currency pairs. Focusing on major currency pairs can help you reduce your risk and improve your trading results.

- **Use Multiple Timeframes**: Using multiple timeframes can provide a broader perspective on the market and help you identify trends and potential entry and exit points. For example, you might use a daily chart to identify the overall trend and a 1-hour chart to identify potential entry points.

- Keep a Trading Journal: Keeping a trading journal can help you track your trades, analyze your performance, and identify areas for improvement. A trading journal can also be a valuable tool for developing and refining your trading strategy.

- Be Patient and Disciplined: Successful forex trading requires patience and discipline. It's important to stick to your trading plan and avoid impulsive trades based on emotions or news headlines.

Forex trading with price action can be a rewarding endeavor, but it requires dedication, discipline, and a solid understanding of the market dynamics. By applying the principles and strategies outlined in this subchapter, you can develop a robust forex trading approach based on price action. Remember, consistent profitability in forex trading is a journey, not a destination. Continuous learning, adaptation, and refinement of your skills are essential for long-term success.

Day Trading with Price Action

Day trading, the practice of buying and selling financial instruments within the same trading day, demands quick decision-making and a keen understanding of market dynamics. Price action trading, with its focus on interpreting raw market data, offers day traders a powerful toolkit to navigate the fast-paced world of intraday trading. This subchapter explores the core principles of day trading with price action, providing insights and strategies to enhance your trading success.

Key Principles of Day Trading with Price Action

- Focus on Short-Term Timeframes: Day traders operate on timeframes ranging from minutes to hours. Price action analysis on charts with intervals like 1-minute, 5-minute, or 15-minute helps identify short-term trends, support and resistance levels, and potential entry and exit points.

- Identify Key Levels: Support and resistance levels act as crucial battlegrounds in day trading. These levels, where prices tend to stall or reverse, can be identified through prior highs and lows, trendlines, or moving averages. Day traders use these levels to anticipate potential turning points and plan their trades accordingly.

- Recognize Chart Patterns: Candlestick patterns like doji, engulfing patterns, and hammer/hanging man offer valuable clues about potential market reversals. Understanding these patterns helps day traders anticipate shifts in momentum and make informed decisions.

- Utilize Volume Analysis: Volume, the number of shares or contracts traded, provides insights into the strength of price movements. Higher volume during breakouts or trend reversals confirms the conviction behind the move, while low volume may indicate a lack of participation and potential false breakouts.

- Manage Risk Effectively: Day trading involves inherent risks. Implementing proper risk management techniques, such as setting stop-loss orders and position sizing based on risk tolerance, is crucial to protect your capital and ensure long-term trading success.

Day Trading Strategies with Price Action

- Breakout Trading: This strategy involves entering a trade when the price breaks out of a defined support or resistance level. Traders identify potential breakout levels and wait for a confirmed break with increased volume before entering the trade. Stop-loss orders are placed below the breakout level for long trades or above the breakout level for short trades.
- Trend Trading: Day traders identify the prevailing trend on a short-term timeframe and look for opportunities to enter trades in the direction of the trend. Trendlines, moving averages, and other technical indicators can be used to confirm the trend and identify potential entry points.
- Reversal Trading: This strategy aims to capture the turning points in the market. Traders look for candlestick patterns, divergence between price and indicators, or exhaustion of a trend to identify potential reversals. Once a reversal is confirmed, traders enter trades in the opposite direction of the prior trend.

- Scalping: Scalping involves taking quick profits from small price movements. Scalpers rely on high-probability setups, tight stop-loss orders, and quick execution to capitalize on intraday volatility.

Example: Day Trading with Price Action

Let's consider an example of day trading the EUR/USD currency pair on a 5-minute chart.

1. **Identify the Trend**: Using trendlines and moving averages, we identify an uptrend on the 5-minute chart.
2. Identify Key Levels: We observe a prior resistance level at 1.1250 and a recent support level at 1.1200.
3. **Look for Entry Signals**: We wait for a pullback to the support level at 1.1200. A bullish candlestick pattern, such as a hammer or engulfing pattern, accompanied by increasing volume, would confirm a potential reversal and provide an entry signal for a long trade.
4. **Set Stop-Loss and Take-Profit**: We place a stop-loss order below the recent swing low, around 1.1180. We set a take-profit target at the prior resistance level of 1.1250, aiming for a 50-pip profit.
5. **Manage the Trade**: We monitor the trade closely and adjust the stop-loss order to breakeven or trail it behind the price as the trade moves in our favor. We exit the

trade if the price breaks below the stop-loss level or reaches the take-profit target.

Tips for Successful Day Trading with Price Action

- Develop a Trading Plan: A well-defined trading plan outlines your strategies, risk management rules, and trade management guidelines. Stick to your plan to avoid impulsive decisions driven by emotions.
- Start Small: Begin with a small trading account and gradually increase your position size as you gain experience and confidence.
- Practice on a Demo Account: Use a demo account to practice your strategies and refine your skills without risking real money.
- Keep a Trading Journal: Record your trades, including entry and exit points, reasons for the trade, and lessons learned. Review your journal regularly to identify strengths and weaknesses in your trading approach.
- Control Your Emotions: Fear and greed can lead to impulsive decisions and losses. Stay disciplined and focus on executing your trading plan.
- Continuously Learn and Adapt: The markets are constantly evolving. Stay updated on market trends, news, and economic events that can

impact your trades. Adapt your strategies as needed to stay ahead of the curve.

Disclaimer: Day trading involves substantial risk and is not suitable for all investors. Past performance is not indicative of future results. Ensure you fully understand the risks involved and seek professional advice if necessary before engaging in day trading.

Stock Trading with Price Action

Stock trading, with its inherent volatility and potential for significant gains, attracts traders from all walks of life. Price action trading offers a unique approach to navigating this dynamic landscape, relying on the direct interpretation of price movements rather than external indicators or news. Let's delve into the intricacies of applying price action strategies to stock trading.

Understanding Price Action in the Stock Market

Price action, in essence, is the study of how prices move over time. In the stock market, this translates to analyzing the fluctuations of a stock's price as depicted on a chart. Candlestick charts are particularly favored in price action trading, as they visually represent the opening, closing, high, and low prices for a specific period. By observing these patterns, traders can identify potential trends, reversals, and key support and resistance levels.

Key Price Action Concepts for Stock Trading

- Support and Resistance: These are crucial levels where price tends to stall or reverse. Support acts as a floor, preventing further price decline, while resistance acts as a ceiling, hindering further price increase. Identifying these levels is pivotal for anticipating potential turning points in a stock's price movement.
- Trendlines: Trends represent the overall direction of price movement. Uptrends are characterized by a series of higher highs and higher lows, while downtrends exhibit lower lows and lower highs. Trendlines, drawn connecting these swing points, provide visual cues about the strength and potential continuation of a trend.
- Candlestick Patterns: Candlestick patterns, formed by individual candles or groups of candles, can offer insights into the balance between buyers and sellers. Patterns like engulfing patterns, doji candles, and hammer candles can signal potential reversals or continuations of existing trends.

- Chart Patterns: Chart patterns, formed by a series of price movements, offer valuable clues about potential future price action. Patterns like head and shoulders, double tops and bottoms, and triangles can indicate trend reversals or continuations, aiding traders in making informed decisions.

Developing a Stock Trading Strategy with Price Action

1. Identify the Trend: The first step is to determine the prevailing trend of the stock. Is it in an uptrend, downtrend, or ranging market? Trend identification helps traders align their strategies with the overall market direction.

2. Identify Key Levels: Locate crucial support and resistance levels on the chart. These levels act as potential entry and exit points, offering opportunities to capitalize on price reversals or breakouts.

3. Look for Candlestick and Chart Patterns: Scan the chart for candlestick patterns and chart patterns that might indicate potential trend reversals or continuations. These patterns provide additional confirmation for trade setups.

4. Plan Your Entry and Exit: Based on the identified trend, key levels, and patterns, determine your entry and

exit points. Define your risk tolerance and set stop-loss orders to protect your capital.

5. Manage Your Trade: Once you've entered a trade, actively manage it by adjusting your stop-loss orders and taking profits at predetermined levels. Stay disciplined and avoid emotional decision-making.

Example: Trading a Breakout with Price Action

Let's consider an example of trading a breakout using price action. Suppose you've identified a stock that has been consolidating within a range for a period. The stock's price is now approaching the upper resistance level of the range. You observe a bullish candlestick pattern forming near the resistance level, indicating potential buying pressure.

In this scenario, you might consider entering a long trade (buy) if the stock's price breaks above the resistance level with strong volume. Your stop-loss order could be placed slightly below the resistance level, protecting you from potential downside risk if the breakout fails. Your profit target could be determined based on the height of the consolidation range or other technical factors.

Advantages of Price Action Trading for Stocks

- Clarity and Simplicity: Price action trading cuts through the noise of external indicators and news, providing a clear and straightforward approach to analyzing price movements.
- Adaptability: Price action strategies can be applied to various stock trading styles, including day trading, swing trading, and position trading.
- Versatility: Price action principles are universal and can be applied across different markets and timeframes.

Challenges of Price Action Trading for Stocks

- Subjectivity: Interpretation of price action patterns can be subjective, requiring practice and experience to develop consistent skills.
- Requires Patience: Price action trading often involves waiting for high-probability setups, requiring patience and discipline.
- Emotional Control: Successful price action trading demands emotional control and the ability to stick to a well-defined trading plan.

Tips for Successful Stock Trading with Price Action

- Start with the Basics: Master the fundamentals of price action, including support and resistance, trendlines, candlestick patterns, and chart patterns.

- Practice on a Demo Account: Before risking real money, hone your skills on a demo account to gain experience and confidence.
- Develop a Trading Plan: Create a well-defined trading plan that outlines your entry and exit criteria, risk management strategies, and trade management techniques.
- Keep a Trading Journal: Maintain a trading journal to track your trades, analyze your performance, and identify areas for improvement.
- Stay Disciplined: Stick to your trading plan and avoid impulsive decisions driven by emotions.

Stock trading with price action offers a powerful approach to navigating the complexities of the market. By focusing on the direct interpretation of price movements, traders can gain valuable insights into potential trends, reversals, and key levels. While it requires practice and discipline, price action trading can provide a rewarding path to achieving consistent profitability in the stock market. Remember, the key lies in mastering the fundamentals, developing a well-defined trading plan, and staying disciplined in your approach.

Cryptocurrency Trading with Price Action

The cryptocurrency market, renowned for its volatility and 24/7 trading, presents unique opportunities and challenges for traders. Price action trading, with its focus on interpreting raw market data, offers a powerful framework to navigate this dynamic landscape. This subchapter will explore the nuances of applying price action strategies to cryptocurrency trading, empowering you to make informed decisions based on market behavior.

Understanding the Cryptocurrency Market

Before diving into specific strategies, it's crucial to grasp the unique characteristics of the cryptocurrency market:

- Volatility: Cryptocurrency prices can experience dramatic swings in short periods. This volatility can amplify both profits and losses, necessitating risk management.
- 24/7 Trading: Unlike traditional markets, cryptocurrency exchanges operate around the clock. This continuous trading creates opportunities but also demands vigilance.
- Market Manipulation: The cryptocurrency market can be susceptible to manipulation due to its

relative youth and lack of regulation. Price action analysis can help identify potential manipulation.

- News and Sentiment: Cryptocurrency prices are heavily influenced by news and sentiment. Staying informed and gauging market sentiment is crucial.

Applying Price Action Principles to Cryptocurrency Trading

- Identify Trends: The first step in price action trading is to identify the prevailing trend. In an uptrend, prices make higher highs and higher lows. In a downtrend, the opposite occurs. Use trendlines and moving averages to confirm trends.
- Support and Resistance: Identify key support and resistance levels. Support is a price level where buying pressure is expected to overcome selling pressure, preventing further price declines. Resistance is a price level where selling pressure is expected to overcome buying pressure, preventing further price increases.
- Candlestick Patterns: Candlestick patterns provide valuable insights into market sentiment. Some common bullish patterns include hammer, engulfing, and morning star. Bearish patterns

include shooting star, hanging man, and evening star.

- Chart Patterns: Chart patterns, such as head and shoulders, double tops and bottoms, and triangles, can signal potential trend reversals or continuations.

Specific Price Action Strategies for Cryptocurrency Trading

1. Trend Following:

- Identify a strong trend using trendlines and moving averages.
- Enter a long position when the price pulls back to a support level in an uptrend.
- Enter a short position when the price rallies to a resistance level in a downtrend.
- Set stop-loss orders below support in an uptrend and above resistance in a downtrend.
- Take profits when the trend shows signs of weakening or reversing.

2. Breakout Trading:

- Identify key support and resistance levels.
- Enter a long position when the price breaks above resistance with strong volume.

- Enter a short position when the price breaks below support with strong volume.
- Set stop-loss orders below the breakout point in a long trade and above the breakout point in a short trade.
- Take profits when the price reaches a new support or resistance level or shows signs of exhaustion.

3. Range Trading:

- Identify a price range where the cryptocurrency is consolidating.
- Buy near support and sell near resistance.
- Set stop-loss orders below support and above resistance.
- Take profits when the price reaches the opposite end of the range.

4. Candlestick Pattern Trading:

- Identify bullish or bearish candlestick patterns.
- Enter a long position after a bullish pattern forms near support or during an uptrend.
- Enter a short position after a bearish pattern forms near resistance or during a downtrend.

- Set stop-loss orders below the low of the candlestick pattern in a long trade and above the high of the candlestick pattern in a short trade.
- Take profits when the price reaches a new support or resistance level or shows signs of exhaustion.

Risk Management in Cryptocurrency Trading

- Position Sizing: Determine the appropriate position size for each trade based on your risk tolerance and account size. A common rule of thumb is to risk no more than 1-2% of your account on any single trade.
- Stop-Loss Orders: Always use stop-loss orders to limit your losses. Place stop-loss orders at logical levels based on support and resistance or recent price action.
- Take-Profit Orders: Use take-profit orders to secure profits. Place take-profit orders at levels where you anticipate the price to encounter resistance or show signs of exhaustion.
- Risk-Reward Ratio: Aim for a favorable risk-reward ratio on each trade. A risk-reward ratio of 1:2 or higher means that your potential profit is at least twice your potential loss.

Additional Considerations for Cryptocurrency Trading

Choosing the Right Exchange: Select a reputable cryptocurrency exchange with high liquidity, low fees, and robust security measures.
Technical Analysis Tools: Utilize technical analysis tools, such as trendlines, moving averages, and oscillators, to complement your price action analysis.
Fundamental Analysis: Stay informed about the latest news and developments in the cryptocurrency space. Fundamental factors can significantly impact prices.
Emotional Discipline: Maintain emotional discipline and avoid impulsive trading decisions. Stick to your trading plan and manage your risk effectively.

Cryptocurrency trading with price action offers a disciplined and effective approach to navigating this volatile market. By understanding market dynamics, identifying key levels, and utilizing price action strategies, you can enhance your trading performance. Remember, successful trading requires continuous learning, practice, and adaptation. Stay informed, manage your risk, and remain disciplined in your approach.

Remember,

Price action trading is a skill that takes time and practice to master.

Start with small position sizes and gradually increase them as you gain experience and confidence.

Always use stop-loss orders to protect your capital.

Don't let emotions dictate your trading decisions.

Continuously learn and adapt your strategies to the ever-changing market conditions.

What Being a Profitable Trader Is All About

Being a profitable trader isn't just about making money in the markets – it's about cultivating a mindset, a skill set, and a lifestyle that allow you to consistently extract gains from the ebb and flow of price action. It's a journey of self-discovery, discipline, and continuous learning, where success is measured not just in profits, but also in the growth and evolution of your trading persona.

The Essence of Profitable Trading

At its core, profitable trading is about achieving a positive expectancy in your trading activities. This means that over a series of trades, the average win should outweigh the average loss, resulting in a net gain over time. However, this simple concept belies the complexity and nuance of what it truly takes to become a consistently profitable trader.

Profitable trading is not about being right all the time; even the most successful traders experience losses. It's about managing risk effectively, cutting losses short, and letting winners run, so that the gains from winning trades more than compensate for the losses from losing trades.

Key Traits of Profitable Traders

- Discipline: Profitable traders adhere to their trading plans and strategies, even when faced with emotional challenges or tempting opportunities. They don't let fear or greed dictate their actions, and they avoid impulsive decisions that can derail their trading goals.

- Patience: The markets don't always offer ideal setups, and profitable traders understand the importance of waiting for high-probability opportunities. They're not afraid to sit on the sidelines and preserve capital until the right moment arises.

- Adaptability: Market conditions are constantly changing, and profitable traders are able to adapt their strategies and approaches accordingly. They're not wedded to any single method or system, and they're always looking for ways to improve their edge.

- Risk Management: Profitable traders prioritize risk management above all else. They understand that preserving capital is essential for long-term success, and they employ techniques such as position sizing and stop-loss orders to limit potential losses.

- Emotional Control: Trading can be a rollercoaster of emotions, from euphoria to despair. Profitable traders are able to manage their emotions and avoid making impulsive decisions driven by fear or greed.

- Continuous Learning: The markets are constantly evolving, and profitable traders are committed to lifelong learning. They stay abreast of market developments, refine their strategies, and seek out new knowledge and insights.

Key Takeaways

- Profitable trading is about achieving a positive expectancy over a series of trades.
- It requires discipline, patience, adaptability, risk management, emotional control, and continuous learning.
- Success in trading is not just about making money, but also about personal growth and development.
- It's a journey, not a destination, and the pursuit of mastery is ongoing.

Next Steps for Becoming a Profitable Trader

1. Develop a Trading Plan: A well-defined trading plan outlines your strategies, risk management rules, and entry/exit criteria. It provides a roadmap for your trading activities and helps you stay disciplined even when emotions run high.

2. Master Risk Management: Understand the importance of preserving capital and implement risk management techniques such as position sizing and stop-loss orders. Never risk more than you can afford to lose on any single trade.

3. Cultivate Emotional Control: Learn to manage your emotions and avoid impulsive decisions driven by fear or greed. Practice mindfulness and meditation techniques to develop mental clarity and focus.

4. Embrace Continuous Learning: The markets are constantly evolving, so commit to lifelong learning. Read books, attend webinars, follow market experts, and analyze your trades to identify areas for improvement.

5. Practice and Refine Your Skills: There's no substitute for experience. Open a demo trading account to practice your strategies and refine your skills without risking real money.

6. Find a Mentor or Community: Connect with experienced traders or join a trading community to learn from others and gain valuable insights.

7. Be Patient and Persistent: Becoming a profitable trader takes time and effort. Don't expect overnight success, and be prepared for setbacks along the way. Stay focused on your goals and keep refining your approach.

Remember, profitable trading is not just about making money; it's about developing a mindset and a skill set that empower you to navigate the markets with confidence and consistency. It's a journey of self-discovery and continuous improvement, where the pursuit of mastery is as rewarding as the financial gains.

Beyond Profits: The Intangible Rewards of Profitable Trading

While financial gains are undoubtedly a primary motivation for traders, the journey to profitability offers many intangible rewards that contribute to a fulfilling and enriching experience.

- Self-Mastery: Trading demands discipline, emotional control, and the ability to make sound decisions under pressure. As you progress on your trading journey, you'll develop these qualities not only in the context of the markets but also in other areas of your life.

- Intellectual Stimulation: The markets are a complex and dynamic ecosystem, and understanding their intricacies requires continuous learning and analysis. Engaging with the markets can be intellectually stimulating, fostering curiosity and a thirst for knowledge.

- Personal Growth: Trading can be a transformative experience, pushing you to confront your limitations and overcome challenges. As you navigate the ups and downs of the markets, you'll develop resilience, adaptability, and a greater sense of self-awareness.

- Financial Independence: Profitable trading can provide a path to financial independence, allowing you to achieve your financial goals and live life on your own terms. This freedom can be empowering and open up new opportunities for personal and professional fulfillment.

Embrace the Journey

Becoming a profitable trader is not an overnight endeavor; it's a lifelong journey of learning, growth, and self-discovery. Embrace the challenges, celebrate the victories, and never stop striving for improvement. Remember, the pursuit of mastery is as rewarding as the financial gains, and the skills and mindset you develop along the way will serve you well in all aspects of your life.

In conclusion, being a profitable trader is about much more than just making money. It's about cultivating a mindset, a skill set, and a lifestyle that allow you to navigate the markets with confidence and consistency. It's a journey of self-discovery, discipline, and continuous learning, where success is measured not just in profits, but also in the growth and evolution of your trading persona. Embrace the journey, stay committed to your goals, and never stop striving for improvement. The rewards, both tangible and intangible, will be well worth the effort.

Happy trading!